Praise for Paul Zarzyski

"Mr. Zarzyski alternates between bluster and lyricism. For the former, he uses lopingly metered stanzas and punch-drunk, self-mythologizing bravura.... But he proves equally adept at meditative free verse...."

The New York Times Book Review

"The Montana poet and bronc rider Paul Zarzyski's diction is as rich as his internal rhymes and alliteration are extravagant."

Thomas West
The Washington Post, Book World.

"In prose literature there are labels such as 'Kafka-esque' and 'Hemingway-esque.' In cowboy poetry there is, or ought to be, 'Zarzyski-esque.' No other '-esques' come close."

Jesse Mullins
American Cowboy Magazine

"Zarzyski's performance style comes on like a rodeo Ferlinghetti...."

Scott Preston
Small Press Review

"Any reading of Zarzyski's complex rhymed and free verse, chocked to the brim, bottom, and edges with mind-racing, overlapping images, is going to tell you that this is a (cowboy) poet with a whole new approach to poetry."

Dale L. Walker
The Rocky Mountain News

STEERING WITH MY KNEES:

Zarzyski Lite

Bangtail
Press

Montana
2014

Also by Paul Zarzyski

Books and Chapbooks

Call Me Lucky (Confluence Press, 1981)
The Make-Up Of Ice (The University of Georgia Press, 1984)
Roughstock Sonnets (The Lowell Press, 1987)
Tracks (The Kutenai Press, 1989)
The Garnet Moon (Black Rock Press, 1990)
I Am Not A Cowboy (Dry Crik Press, 1994)
All This Way For The Short Ride (Museum of New Mexico Press, 1996)
Blue-Collar Light (Red Wing Press, 1998)
Wolf Tracks On The Welcome Mat (Carmel Publishing / Oreanabooks, 2003)
Becoming Flight (Heavy Duty Press, 2004)
51: 30 Poems, 20 Lyrics, 1 Self-Interview (Bangtail Press, 2011)

Spoken-Word Recordings

Ain't No Life After Rodeo (Horse Sense Music,1992)
Words Growing Wild (Jim Rooney Productions, 1999)
The Glorious Commotion Of It All (Jim Rooney Productions, 2003)
Rock-n-Rowel (Open Path Music, 2006)
Collisions Of Reckless Love (Open Path Music, 2006)

STEERING WITH MY KNEES

Published in the United States by

Bangtail Press
P. O. Box 11262
Bozeman, MT 59719
www.bangtailpress.com

Cover art and all interior illustrations by Larry Pirnie.

IN MEMORY OF RIPLEY AND RICHARD HUGO—
With gratitude for all the laughs at 2407 Wylie Ave.

TABLE OF CONTENTS

1

THEY TRAVEL IN TWOS

THE GUNS OF PROVOLONE

HUMMOCKING ERUMPENT

COWPOKE COSMOS HIGHS

MY CATTYWAMPUS NOGGIN

SWIMMIN' THE COW*BOY* FOUNTAIN OF YOUTH

MY HOPALONG GODIVA

CHIANTI *SALUTES!*

NO-LAUGHING-GAS-IN-HELL MAD

ROARING WITH METAPHORICAL FIRE

"God is a comedian playing to an audience too afraid to laugh."
François-Marie Arouet—Voltaire

"Dying is easy. Comedy is difficult."
Actor Edmund Gwenn (on his deathbed)

"From the moment I picked your book up until I laid it down,
I was convulsed with laughter. Someday I intend reading it."
Julius Henry "Groucho" Marx

INTRODUCTION

The Risible Poetic Crazy Bone in the Elbow of the Inner Ear

Call Me Lucky, to invoke the title of my first poetry chapbook, because I've mostly reveled, throughout my decades, in a humorous youth, and I sometimes still do, albeit with far less ease—especially so when launching the serious mission of infusing this "youthful humor" into the galactic components of a poem. I garner little poetic lift-off from the "golden years." Watching my body collapsing at sixty-two is damn near as lachrymose as watching, at five, Old Yeller getting shot. I loathe that feeble adage of suggested duality, that "it (aging) beats the alternative." As in, there's only one other option? And it is not likely conducive to the continuation of poetic output? In a porcine derriere, says defiant I. Give me a break. Give me the bigger, Chinese / Korean / Thai / American restaurant menu from which to choose. Give me the return of Steve Jobs in his iTimeMachine to unveil his latest innovation, the iLife! Hell, Bartender-God, in the din of the clock's accelerated tick-down toward "closing time," just give this thanatopsis-obsessed, windmill-tilting Don Quixote another drink. For to quote my brother Gary quoting a sign on the wall of his favorite watering hole, "Alcohol: because no great story (or poem!) ever began with someone eating a salad."

All swagger and bullshit braggadocio aside, I confess that the ironic fuse igniting this compilation of forty years of humorous / silly / goofy poetic focuses was actually lit by too much time jousting with real, *non*-windmill, demons—lit by an urgency to break out of that gloaming. My dad was diagnosed with a terminal disease in late December, 2007, and died the following October. I was at my mother's bedside in August of 2010 as she shed her final tear and took her last breath. Since then, too many friends have battled and lost to diseases which I believe we, as a supposed civilized, intelligent species, would have conquered by now, had we opted to invest more of our trillions into medical science rather than into military science and the armaments thereof. Speaking of the latter, Liz and I, sitting on the sofa a while back in front of the LG (Life's Good?) TV with dinner plates in our laps, wept into our leftovers as the parents of children lost in the Sandy Hook Elementary massacre discussed with *60 Minutes* interviewer Scott Pelley how they were coping. As my dear Italian mother would have proclaimed had she been watching with us, "*Toooo* sad." And what I sensed between the lines of those interviewees' heart-writhing expressions was, "We do whatever we can to place one breath, one heartbeat, one footstep, one agonizing memory, one toe-hold nuance of life's ballet, one slow-motion iota of time, after another." Not a single parent alluded to, let alone mentioned, humor or laughter or levity as even the most minuscule tincture to their anodynes. The term "funny" will likely never again register in their lives as it once did prior to their devastations.

Which is all to suggest, ever-so-humbly, that I have indeed felt fortunate over the past months for the infusion of merriment brought on by the compiling of these poems. They've afforded me a lift from the darker quagmires of my psyche—all thanks and praise to the bombastic, vociferous noise I'm fond of stirring up, solely for the fun of it, on the page. Fun with words—for me, akin to hours spent on the shrink's divan; for impecunious me, cheap therapy—self-medication. I could never have imagined, while writing one-by-occasional-one these ridiculous testimonials over the past four decades, that someday I'd be leaning on them again, this time as a unit, for stability—clinging to them like packing-peanut *cucaracha* life buoys in a monsoon. But here I am doing exactly that, and, moreover, inviting you aboard for, as far-fetched as it may sound, a poetic, magical realism trip into my *Life of Pie*?

As for the writing itself, trust me: Poetry-funny—especially poetry-funny *ha-ha*! (although that is not the ambition of the majority of these works)—is no easy feat. I was fortunate to cut my poetic teeth on the persona works of esteemed poet Paul Zimmer, whose early books conveyed one of the most simple, essential tenets of humor, a willingness to (cow)poke fun at oneself—"Zimmer, Drunk and Alone, Dreaming of Old Football Games," "Zimmer's Head Thudding Against the Blackboard," "Zimmer, the Luckless Fisherman, Dreams He is a Fish," "Zimmer Envying Elephants":

> ...I'd like to thud amply around
> For a hundred years or more,
> Stuffing an occasional tree top
> Into my mouth, screwing hugely for
> Hours at a time, gaining weight,
> And slowly growing a few hairs.

I must have deduced the obvious logic of the correlation early on—if Paul Zimmer, poet, *ergo* why not poet Paul Zarzyski? One of my first-ever attempts (1972)—"Zarzyski, Not Exactly Wild Bill Hickok"—is included here. As is my maiden waltz into cowboy poetry— "Zarzyski Meets the Copenhagen Angel." Zarzyski mimics Zimmer—high jinks fertilizing the way for further high jinks. I'll say it again, however—"Poetry-funny is *no* easy feat." Thank goodness, therefore, for imagistic hyperbole to the extreme power; thank goodness for exaggerated splashes of exaggerated rhyme and slant rhyme; thank goodness for the often frivolous, ratcheted effect of jazz-scatted stacked adjectives; thank goodness (again and again, *and* again) for the Rodney Dangerfield-esque gift of self-deprecation, which most any bathroom mirror ought to prompt out of most any stand-up poet worth his observational salt. (I, by the way, have the mother of all bathroom mirrors, complete with eight—count them, *eight*— hundred-watt *non*-vanity lights illuminating the most obvious butt of ridicule in the room, yours truly.) And *especially* thank goodness for the oftentimes brutally crude, puissance of my pulchritudinous nymphomaniac Muse oozing her word-music-juices through sensual tattoos. Which segues beautifully to the debt of gratitude I owe the Musical Universe, as well, for imbuing our lingo with its voluptuous phonetics, especially the *OO* sound, to which I sw*OO*ned, madly in lust, during my very first phonics lesson.

Not only is poetry-funny difficult, but, to place a far more arduous spin on that difficulty, the music of humor is *not* universal. The DNA helix of the funny, or crazy, bone varies from ear to ear, from sensibility to sensibility. As a youngster, I remember my dad telling the same dozen jokes—ad nauseam, I suppose, to some, but to a boy of seven or eight, with great comedic success: "Do you know what that white stuff in chicken shit is called? Chicken shit!" I could never understand why Mom didn't laugh.

Since humor, therefore, cannot obviously be calculated or formulated or preordained (I'm guessing two of my current favorite comedic writers of their own stand-up material, Lewis Black and Sarah Silverman, as well as my all-time fave, George Carlin, would agree) all I can do is to try to amuse *myself* into even a thin smile and then hope to invite, to *incite,* those in the presence of the work to join in, to sing along with me in the shower, so to speak. In the midst of our symbiotic duet (on the page), or chorus (on the stage), should the audience blossom beyond thin smiles into grins, chuckles, or outright guffaws, I will graciously genuflect to the gods of chance, happenstance, dumb luck.

Which brings us—don't ask me "how?"—to Mae West's dictum, "It's hard to be funny when you have to be clean." Not always, perhaps, but every now and then?

Steering with my Knees is, for me, the quintessential *ars poetica* metaphor. My anti-anxiety-pill-popping guardian angel, who, incidentally, posed for Edvard Munch's "The Scream," knows only too well how many times I have lived this title "doing 80" in my beloved 1971 viper-red Monte Carlo—while scribbling words, far too hot for memory to handle, across the envelope of an overdue bill or into my sweaty left palm. Or, perhaps hairier yet, lived it aboard a 1200 pound bucking horse kicking 16 dizzying different directions at once. Which is to say, may the covens of sozzled Muses hoist their smoldering goblets of dirty martinis in tribute to reckless abandon, especially on the page, the canvas—anything less, offering nowhere near enough the poetic longitude and latitude required for me to cross over and / or to tap into creativity's infinities.

In closing, thank you for lending me not only your Wild Bill Shakespearean ears, but also your *Bizarzyski*-zany crazy bones in the elbows of said "loaned ears." Thank you for steering with *your* knees while reading these poems and, thereby, for humoring *me*.

October, 2013

ARTIST'S STATEMENT

Anytime Mr. Z. invites me to contribute to one of his creations, I jump at the opportunity to collaborate with one of my dearest friends. When he told me this collection of his poetry would be on the "lite" side, I was enthused, even though my work within the body of the book would be reproduced in black and white.

My challenge in getting started with the images was convincing "the kid" in me that working in black and white would be fun. The kid didn't buy into it at first because using color is the only way I can get him to come out and play. Eventually I conned him into the project by doing all the preliminary work in color, and then for the final phase of the creation, converting the images to black and white.

The images are done within a collage concept using digital software to manipulate the individual elements, which I've taken primarily from existing paintings, field sketches, and photographs. Although the process excited the "intellectual" side of me, the kid isn't convinced that the last phase of the image-making was playful enough due to the absence of color. This experience, however, has encouraged me to pursue more black and white projects. I've often recognized and admired black and white paintings of other artists. Maybe the kid will eventually learn to do the same.

Pirnie

Into Youth's Oblivion Cool

BINGO IN THE CHURCH BASEMENT

"I-19—under the I, 19—I-19,"
the Knights of Columbus grand pooh-bah
crooned into the mike, his Sinatra-
suave mimicry pole-axed by a cross
between a Richard Boone and Bogie voice. Zinc
pennies and buttons, pinto beans
and tiddlywinks rattled from tins
down the long rows of tables, tarantula hands
of mustachioed Italian women
playing, with one arm, umpteen cards each,
while their off hands worked
rosaries coiled in their laps—silence,
another number, a choir of sighs, and then
the crescendo of mutterings
and markers clicking into place, until

"under the N, 32…" **"Bingo!"**
blew a hole through the bogus air
of the faithful. "Rich Mrs. Morgainti again?"
I whined my boy-of-eight complaint
amid a room filled with envy,
a venial bit of tenth commandment tilt
thriving those Friday nights
in the holy casino, where we flocked
praying we'd hit it big
to the patron saint of high stakes,
while God, watching us, as always,
through His fish-eye lens
from the chancel upstairs, called down—
number-by-Mafioso-number—
His crooked shots to the pit boss, Guido.

For Paul Sturgul

14

RIDING DOUBLE—16 AND BEATING THE HEAT

"...continually
Drunk on the wind in my mouth,
Wringing the handlebar for speed,
Wild to be wreckage forever."
James Dickey
"Cherrylog Road"

She loved my black Triumph
motorcycle, flamed orange
and chromed, my Brando jacket,
all nine zippers half-unzipped—
leather and chest hair
her long-nailed fingers prowled
like barracuda. Doing 95
through a 92 degree wave,
I loved her breasts
flexed and churning
into the muscles of my back,
loved our flesh-and-metal duet, sheer
defiance of double yellow lines
between us and the abandoned
dancehall we roared to
to quell our heat. In rebellion
against all law—mortal or God's,
death to gravity—we staked the physical
against pure physics. We throttled
wide open, torrid on lust, hopped-up
on the four-stroke's solo
double-tongued through straight-pipes,
fired on two bits worth of fuel. Hell,
we made our own damn breeze,
we kamikazed the heat, our fevers
breaking into youth's oblivion cool.

HURLEY HIGH

Though the nuns had dubbed us crusaders
in the war against puberty, we gladly lost
to testosterone and Pabst
Blue Ribbon rumbling in our blood. We sang
the dirty version of "Louie Louie"
gung ho with elocution
we learned from Coach Wick,
WW II English-teaching marine
who recited "The Locker Room Charge
of the Light Brigade" like God or Lombardi Himself
pounding home to Moses how to block
for the power sweep. We cruised
the drag of a no-horse town
lit by aurora borealis and beer-sign
neon twisted into images
rioting inside us, our hearts
like tin cups raked
across our ribs. What terrific lust
we mixed with hope, with first sex
to tenor sax and electric guitar—
brass horns and chromed cars
we cocked our smooth faces toward
while combing full heads of hair. We lived for hits,
six-packs, and the third deuce
kicking-in down the s-curved river road
to Litzer's, where we flashed
our fake IDs across the bar at Blind Ed,
blew Lucky Strike smoke rings and rocked
wild on raw fun, just to pass
for 18 on a Friday night in 1966,
when Friday night meant living,
and living meant sinning till dawn.

SCARS POETICA

Brushed over with arm hair, the nickel-cigar scars
I've not told a sober soul about
since the sixties, until now, until finding myself
hanging by a hemp thread
between the devil and the deep blue sea,
(the blank page at 3 a.m.),
so desperately in need of a poetic fix
I'd welcome it from a telemarketer
pushing vertical chicken cookers
or even a graveyard shift Jehovah's Witness
ringing my bells—these scars
(I started to show and tell)
looking like smallpox inoculations
stabbed by W. C. Fields playing some ice pick-
wielding demonic school nurse,
these scars are the mimickings of a biker
flick in which two nasty, nasty tough guys,
their forearms like a couple of USDA-stamped
smoked hams pressed against one another
on the mahogany bar, place a dog-turd stogy
evenly into the V of muscles
twitching not even a little.
                              To this day, I cringe
with flashbacks of that red-eyed gut-tester
making our nerve centers flicker and buzz
with Blatz Beer neon, all fail-safe
warning lights, at crazy 18, blazing
long after the point of no return or *give*,
after the stench of our flesh searing
sent weaker-intestined patrons
retching out the door—the bartender, holding
fast with his yellow snot-rag
pressed over his face, one-arming to us

pitcher after pitcher of fire-retardant Schlitz
we guzzled quicker than he could
shuffleboard them
down the bar, our smoldering
stogies eventually going cold,
and the joint, Litzer's, blowing smoke
rings out its opened windows
as we blistered big and ugly.
                                        For months,
our arms oozed like Vesuvius, seethed, scabbed over,
festered again until the grayish blue and pink
paisley sheen began to fade
beneath long sleeves we'd roll up
to show off our medallions
of machismo at Barnabo's Pool Hall
after school.
                        Thirty-something summers later,
they still itch and flake dead skin—white sand
islands in the stream of deep tan. None of us
won or lost, or croaked, so far
as I know, from melanoma. Nobody
landed a starring Hollywood role
in *Chopper Mania*. No one got laid
a day sooner than he would have gotten laid
anyway. And now, as I muse
on the fiery rendering of these scars
more closely, didn't they come into being
just a little like writing poetry?

For Dave Alvin—After Reading
Any Rough Times Are Now Behind You

ZARZYSKI MEETS THE COPENHAGEN ANGEL

Her Levis, so tight
I can read the dates on dimes
in her hip pocket. Miles City,
a rodeo Saturday night.
She smiles from a corner bar stool,
her taut lower lip, white and puffed,
pigtails braided like bronc reins.
She leads the circuit, chasing cans,
a barrel racer in love with her horse,
her snuff, and a 16-second run.
We dance close to LeDoux's "Daydream Cowboy."
"I'm Zarzyski, rhymes with bar-whiskey,"
I tell her—"a lover, a fighter,
a Polish bareback bronc rider."
And these Copenhagen kisses jump and kick
higher than ol' Moonshine, himself.

For Debbie Moore

RIDING DOUBLE-WILD

Lyric Precursor to "Double Wild"
Recorded by Wylie Gustafson

She's a motorcycle sister
He's a bareback bronco twister
They're ridin' double-wild 'cross the West.
She's Mescalero Indian
He's full-blooded Paladin
Runnin' on a buck's worth of Texaco high-test.

She drives that bike full-throttle
There's still a half-full bottle
Of mescal in her studded saddlebags.
He spurs those buckers crazy
But now he's laid-back lazy
As *her* batwing chaps are flappin' just like flags.

    Cowboy grit, Apache pride,
    Wild hearts and minds collide
    In a fiery mix of youth and speed and steel.
    "Hell on horses, hell on women,"
    The West has changed, boys, look what's comin',
    Rearin'-up and roarin' toward you on one wheel.

John B. Stetsons and stampede strings
Sterling skull and crossbone earrings
Moonlight gleaming off her buckrein braids.
Sleekly forked to mean machine
Sinewy meets serpentine
Meets 200 proof of red-eyed renegades.

Leather jacket skinny-dippers
His fingers swim through all her zippers
Her pores like Braille across her tattooed neck.
Sipping from that beaded rose
Its stem of thorns beneath her clothes—
What he whispers in her ear could cause a wreck.

They're both living high on ridin'
Never circling or backslidin'
Get your holts, pop the clutch, skyward bound.
Pinto stallion, black and chrome,
Painted metal, flesh and bone—
It's not always true that what goes up comes down.

Cowboy grit, Apache pride,
Wild hearts and minds collide
In a fiery mix of youth and speed and steel.
Broncs and choppers, who'd have guessed it,
West meets West, boys, manifested,
Rearin'-up and roarin' toward you on one wheel.

For Larry Pirnie—In Tribute to Your
Triple-Wild Image on Page 26

WHY I LIKE *BUTTE!*—*OR,* "HOW
SHE GOIN' TODAY, *JUST?*"

From the Gogebic Iron Range—"shaking ground," in Ojibwa—
across open range of the Plains Indian
turned cowboy, from Dad riding the cage for 8-
hour pick-and-shovel, double-jack-and-blast shifts
thirty-six levels below surface in the Montreal stopes,
to me winning more than his monthly wage
for 8-second buckin' horse rides
aboard Spitfire and Coors Light
in Butte, America, I know my true home is
where ethnic hearts of blue-collar folk
mine and smelt hot blood from veins
then pour it into their arteries
like molten ore. *BUTTE!* With its rambunctious
shamrock-curvy girls, who danced, until the last
Tony Lama'd dogs died,
with us rodeo rebels—jitterbugging from the Helsinki
on the lip of The Pit, through swing shift
breakfast at the M&M, to break of day
red beers at Maloney's. *BUTTE!* The one and only
arena I did not bite the dirt in—never
dusted, pile-drived, or drilled—where I prayed
Hail Marys long before the Mountaintop
Madonna, "Our Lady of the Rockies," The Butte Guadalupe,
beamed down upon the buckin' chutes—
prayed the same "Hail Mary
full of grace" I pleaded as a child wanting
to be spared a lifetime in the mines. *BUTTE!*
With its phone book ringing with the familiar
ilk of Ginty Fontecchio, Reino Peltomaki, Pupsy Savant,
Eino Aho handles I grew up with
in Hurley, Wisconsin—Mick, Dago, Cousin-Jack,
Polack, Finn, syncopated names
stout with thick sinewy consonants and loud

vowels musical to the tongue's lit-fuse-
to-powder touch. ***BUTTE!*** Cold spot
of the nation every other February day
but hot come mid-March
when even Her beer blossoms green in the warmth
of corned beef and cabbage, pasty pie and riotous
laughter of Her people—O'Boyle, McTavish,
Zolinski, Aho, Maki, Antonolli—all for one,
one for all, on Saint Paddy's Day. ***BUTTE!*** Raising hell
and placing a Blarney Stone beneath it. ***BUTTE!***
Holier than hell and *damn* proud
of it. ***BUTTE!*** Hell to drive through
but oh, *what heaven* to spend the night in
       BUTTE!

For Tudo (Arturo) Stagnoli, John Powers,
Susan Fogarty-Schwab—and to the
Eternal Spirit of Poet, Ed Lahey

THE POET & THE PICKER

On that bright night when Music gives
a lift to lonesome Poetry
hitchhiking 40 light years of bad road,
it isn't long before they find out stars
are nothing less than hot-note
reflections off polished chrome.

Cruising the cosmos in Music's '57
Chevy drop-top Bel Air—
past the Mobil Station's red Pegasus,
past rebel-rousing rodeo roadhouses,
sock hops and outdoor picture shows—
they drive in to The Bucking Horse Moon
where a sweet-wheels-and-sassy-chassis blonde
carhop in a letter sweater
skates them a brace of cherry Cokes
and blows the bitchin'est ever
Bazooka Bubble Gum
bubble as she swoons
over their deep blue tuck-n-roll
interior, their rock-n-rowel
duet purring and purring her
ponytailed, gum-smacking Wolfman Jack lingo.

Play, Duane Eddy, play
your candy-apple-red Gretsch
electric guitar. Hold you own boss heart
cradled in your arms—the body's wild one
busting free and taking us
to the place it hides
the diamonds, youth
ditched piece-by-jeweled-piece
in life's richest heist. Tonight, in our 50s,
racing like quasars in reverse
toward teenager infinity, you pick a single string
and I know my words—pitching woo,
moving closer to your notes at the center
court of the Milky Way gymnasium—
waltz with the prettiest girls in this world.

For Duane

Under The Wicked One's Dash

MONTE CARLO EXPRESS—
POST OFFICE BOX 258, 15.3 MILES HOME

I've checked fence doing 80 in a low-rider
Chevrolet springing the borrow pit
like a pack mule that hates crossing
running water. The torture is too much
when a week's worth of mail—stacked
beside me like a high school majorette
beckoning with her baton
decades back when this car was showroom new—
presses against me. I could never wait and still
can't wait to open what's personal. Steering
with my knees, jackknife gleaming in my lap,
the wheel tilted down full—The Monte, a roulette
ball blur hugging hot asphalt—I shuffle
through the stack and gamble
once again on 8 miles of 2-lane
straightaway. I Frisbee bills and all business
glassine-windowed envelopes,
in which we poets never receive checks,
over the suicide seat headrest, toss
junk mail to the floor-mat collage
on the shotgun side, stick love letters
between my teeth, and maybe I'm better off
not having tasted perfume
for years. *Esquire*, slicker than a hot plastic
sack of slimy grunion, slithers and slides
over, under, and between the seats
leaving its Stetson Cologne scent
like a madam's tomcat mascot marking his turf
on two-for-one night
in a cowboy brothel. Ol' Monte drifts
left across the double yellows on a hill
then right, into the shoulder brome, seed heads
whipping the wheel wells clean, dust swirling

in the side mirror, the Day-Glo
rubber fish in place of plastic Jesus
dashing for the stuntmen grasshoppers
suctioned to the windshield,
their front paws clasped in prayers
that must have saved us from the bridge
abutment already signed
with 4 white crosses for those who did not
quite
       make
           this
              curve
because of booze, because of snooze, because of
tire or tie rod act-of-God failure
of car or heart, or the piss-poor
penmanship of a good friend
loving me almost to cursive death with this letter.

For Rick and Carole DeMarinis,
and to Teddy-Bob "Roadkill Penmanship" Waddell

"THE CAR THAT BROUGHT YOU HERE STILL RUNS" *

* From Richard Hugo's "Degrees of Gray in Philipsburg"

It takes more than gasoline and gumption
to get you to Zortman—more
than whimsy or a wild inkling
to rekindle history. It takes a primal prairie
kinship with Old Man Winter, with Napi
hunkering in sunless gulches, a longing
for short Fourth of July parades, the best-
kept-secret café with a waitress
who commutes 50 miles from Malta—
"big city with its 5 p.m. rush minute,"
she quips. What can anyone say in words
that Charles Marion Russell has not
narrated in paint. Little Rockies, Larb Hills,
predator versus prey versus wind
still give this Indian-cowboy
landscape its animation.
                                    Your three eggs
jiggling explicitly over-easy, hash browns crisp,
rough-cut slabs of bone-in ham,
one pancake seat-cushioned over its own plate,
make you wish you'd packed
your camera's wide-angle lens. Panned
first, then filtered, the coffee is
as impasto-thick as the décor—
local art collaged in barnwood frames
above faux-brick wainscoting.
                                    Lucky—
the 11 a.m. lull all to yourselves—
you are, for once, simply where you need
to be. Do not ponder why. Do not
ask the waitress what brought her here

from Seattle. The wall clock is not
locked in *pause.* Thus, you better be
willing to revel in this living limbo,
this muffling of drumroll death.
                              Muse
over your food. Ruminate,
while chewing, on each tooth's name—
incisor, canine, bicuspid, molar. Salute
the taste buds, bitter to sweet,
as you clean your plate, pony up,
inch your way out of town
with a groan, your heartstrings, taut
lariats stretched to whatever
rogue lodestar pulled you into this
still-shot of Montana past—grass ropes
aching to hold for only so long.

For Dick and Ripley, and in tribute to
Frances McCue's literary masterpiece,
The Car That Brought You Here Still Runs.

THE DAY BEELZEBUB GAVE
HIS JEZEBEL A HOTFOOT…

…it was 52 below zero in Butte, Montana
where they were marooned, after the hellhole
it took them an eternity to drive up through
froze over, their fire-engine-red Firebird
vapor-locking to a frigid halt
as they unwittingly drove beneath Our Lady
Of The Rockies—Snow White with an attitude,
all ninety blessed feet and eighty steel virgin tons of her
standing vigil over the Berkeley Pit.
                                    Red,
the mechanic at Red's Firebrand Texaco
tells the devil, "She ain't a-firin', no spark,
Bub, and I'll be go-to-hell
if I can savvy what the hitch is
in your git-along-little-dogie,"
not knowing just how "go-to-hell" he'll truly be
if he doesn't get humorless Lucifer
back on the road, pronto. But how in hell
was Red supposed to know? The shrewd master
of disguise—tail, horns, cloven feet,
pointy ears and all—looked purt-near like most
everyone else bundled-up and ruddy-jowled
on just another colder-than-hell Butte
December afternoon.
                        "Hell-o, *HELL*-O!"
Red heard ol' Diablo losing his cool
on the phone, deader than hell
for the seventh day straight. "Lord only knows
when they'll get the lines back up—ought to
change their handle from Ma Bell to Hell's Bells,"
quips Red from underneath the hotrod
up to Satan, so much fire in his eyes
Red no longer needs his trouble light, nor does he

fully comprehend the severity of his faux pas
as he rubs it in doubly deep with his
emphatic refrain, "Lord *only* knows!" Followed-up with:
"this cold spell sure has been raisin' holy hell
around here this Christmas, and…Jee-*zuz* H. Key-*rice*-st
on a crooked crutch…." Red didn't miss a beat,
oblivious to how timely was his exclamation,
Beelzebub's mood suddenly up-swung
with Red's good news of the netherworld's
crippled-up nemesis.
                              "Hell-a-looya
and here's to ya, my fumin' friend—I *by God*
got your pickle pegged: your cataclysmic conundrum
mustta rubbed against your firewall, overheated,
and burnt your muffler valve
all to hell. Hope you're packin' a fire
extinguisher in this beast. Helluvanote, Bub,
but *thank heaven* I just happen to have the parts
to git you the hell-n-gone outta here." Beelzebub bit
hard his barbed tongue to keep from saying
"WHAT A GODSEND!"
                              By now,
Beelzebub is in dire need
of a Hades Boilermaker—a case of Heet
gasoline deicer and a three-fingers' (all he's got)
shot of Habanero Chile Pepper Schnapps. Back,
at long last, to the B&B (he thought it stood for
Beelzebub and Babe) he finds his beloved
bedazzling behemoth redhead buried
eyeball (she's only got one) deep
beneath electric blankets turned on all the way
to HOT. She's snoring her erotic snore
which brings ol' Beelzebub's blood to a brisk
molten lava boil until he can't
say "no" to his own temptations

when he catches a glimpse of her horny yellow
foot sticking through the wrought iron rails
and arousing him all to hell.
                          That day
Beelzebub gave his Jezebel a hotfoot,
the matchbook read "River Styx
Hot Springs—Nether World," and "Oh *God!*
Oh *God!*" did Beelzebub's Jezebel ever have one
jump-start of an orgasmic jolt
that made the San Andreas Fault
(their second favorite vacation spot)
quaking 9.8 on the Richter Scale
seem like an infinitesimal jiggle, a flinch,
a dust mite's climax.
                          As they jubilantly sped
out of Butte, two helmeted apparitions
dressed horn-to-hoof in Halloween orange
and packing firearms for the late elk hunt
passed them on Hellcat snowmobiles
making Beelzebub lonesome for his own
florescent bed of coals. And you can bet
your most diabolic act of defiance—
like that magnetic glow-in-the-dark
Saint Christopher medal sly ol' Red slapped up
under the Wicked One's dash—
that not even 666 eons of global warming,
complete with 666 *hell* niños
plus two free passes to the Helsinki bathhouse
could ever tempt Beelzebub
to make his Jezebel, Helena, *come…here…again.*

*In memory of Trish Pedroia, who grinned
devilishly at this one.*

THE CAPIT*AL* OF MONTANA (A "FOUND POEM")

Picture her printing this in the skimpy margins
of a dollar bill—cockeyed George
cracking, under magnification,
the semblance of a devilish grin—
a blissful gal, I suspect,
donning that smile that time-travels
a man's, *or* woman's, fantasies
back to first stirrings as she exclaims
her unabashed, indelible, punctuated
debt of erogenous gratitude
beginning above, and parallel to, the words
FEDERAL RESERVE NOTE:

Thanks for the nasty all-nighter, never thought it
(hard 90 degrees right)
could be that *GRRREAT*—
(bottom-dollar George spun bottoms-up)
 OH YEAH! Love you—Helena's Hot Waitress.

      Now, I don't know
        about I-*duh*-ho,
but in greenback Montana, boys and girls,
that's what we call "making change for a five."

                    For Buzzy Vick—Montana's
                    "Hot Waitress" at Heart

MAKING HER DAY

When Dorothy, queen of the drive-thru
bank tellers, looks cyborg-bored
going about her ad nauseam rote
goldfish-in-a-bowl motions, I whip
my viper-red Monte Carlo lowrider,
its shark's-snout hood with chrome sneer,
into a U-turn, head-on against the one-way grain,
punch it into the lane most occupied, brake,
slide-n-stretch across the long front seat
to just barely roll with fingertips into my palm
the Plexiglas cylinder. I load
its aptly-calibrated chamber with two
Pabst Blue Ribbon cartridges
just to marvel at the magical
swallow-and-belch
suction as they're vacuumed
subterraneanly into the money bunker,
badda-boom, faster than a jackalope
pops up out of a hemp patch
just north of the Wyoming border. Dorothy,
corneas drowning in the aqueous
humor of computer numerals,
her right hand on automatic pilot,
plucks the tube and hefts it
like a dumbbell curl
up to the plate glass. "Feels like Paul
is *cashing in* his piggy bank *again*,"
she quips over the PA, to the aghast

muffler-exhaust-asphyxiated customers
slack-jawed in a bottlenecked
standstill shattering of their cast-
in-granite comfort zone. Oh, and how
it makes *my* day to bust out
iconoclastically into most any
only-in-Montana shenanigan, just to blow
the entropic dust off the status quo,
to buck the humdrum. Dumbstruck,
at first blush, by my brewski deposit,
Dorothy, inside her cubicle's picture tube,
breaks into her Land of Oz good-witch croon
"*thannkk* you, *Paulll!*"—not once,
as she booted up for work that morning,
banking on this "yellow brick road" liquid lucre
gratuity, this barley soup duet,
this *Vitamin B* sudsy luncheon supplement,
every bit as enchanting as two
Munchkin-Land ruby slippers
slipping magically out of her pneumatic tube.

For Dorothy Herman

HOT LOAVES IN THE MONTE CARLO

In part, because Christ chose hearty bread
to complement both the fishes and the wine, because
Charlie Russell named his favorite horse
Monte, loved Christmas, and Great Falls is
Kid Russell's hometown,
I place the opened paper bags of hot
Great Harvest Bakery
three-pound round loaves—like nests
snuggled together
tighter than muffins in a tin—
on the saddle blanket seat covers,
then nose ol' Monte into the Christmas
Eve blizzard. With a "Ho! Ho! Ho!-ski,"
a Polish-Italian-Santa hug or handshake,
and a "thanks for the friendship," I deliver
this savory cranberry-orange
bread to the gracious women
working the Saint Vinny and Sally Ann thrifts,
to the father-son mechanics—Monte's
sawbones faves—of West-Side Sinclair,
to the drive-thru teller at Stockman Bank,
Dorothy, who did not call in the cavalry
(*thank* the patron saint of foolish stunts)
that day I, brandishing matched cap pistols,
rode up to her bullet-proof window
in my stick-'em-up bandana. Oh, yes,
and to George the barber, who at least *tries*
to give me the ol' "trim the sides, fill the middle"
vanity cut. And to the One-Hour
Martinizing husband-wife team
working their miracles on my risque
girlie ties stained with amoeboid
myriads of mixed-drink
montages from the *Mr. Boston
Deluxe Bartender's Guide,*

Apricot Ladies to Zaza Cocktails
to everything in between—you bet,
especially the *Mai Tai*! And, most
rejoicing of all, to those homebound, snowed-in—
long-timers, wisdom-keepers—who I have
not once, since growing up
among the gnarled, blue-collar elderly,
looked in the eye without seeing
myself. To Violet, coming 90,
exclaiming, "heck, ya can't have summer
all winter long, ya know!" And to Barbara,
so cozy in her 1960 sky-blue trailer house
she shares with Lonesome,
the night-crawler-gulping tropical frog, his skin
white as, yes, *snow*. All afternoon,
rubbing with my Christmassy red
and yellow Handy Andy chore gloves
portholes in Monte's steamed-up
windshield, I peer out from within
this vintage Chevrolet ornament
I fantasize dangling from some luminous tree
amidst Orion's stars and tinseled
Betelgeuse nebulas. "Laughing
all the way," in a three-fifty-horse
hardtop sleigh, I, the last of the loaves,
steeped in my doughy cologne, glide
home through big lazy hypnotic flakes
drifting me back to 1950's Wisconsin
Christmases I am *so* lucky,
maybe even blessed, to catch
sentimental glimpses of myself
still believing in as a kid.

For Pete Rysted, and in
Memory of George Skaer

The Meaning Of Fur-Bearing Life

LINGUISTICS

Spitting a mouthful of clothespins
like a goalie spitting teeth, the first time
Mother strung curse words with God's name
in vain, she was hanging sheets,
the clean smell of 20 Mule Team Borax
on a warm July morning. With a knack
for not letting them sweep the ground,
she pulled the long linens—still layered in esses,
compressed and heavy from the Maytag's wringer—
and stretched them, like saltwater taffy,
unfurling and pinning them to the lines
in one fluid motion. Behind her back, Jack,
my pet crow, perched on the wicker basket, shot
a whitewashed stream across those sheets,
and then, not knowing holy hell
Italian-style, screeched back at her
a Heckle-n-Jeckle laugh
amid the feathered fracas of mother's slapstick
slap shot kick that came *this close*
to putting poor Jack, a black blur
of raucous puck, into cartoon orbit.

Jack, box-office-hit
fledgling that Leonard Zaleski filched
from the crown of a hundred-foot pine—cawed
constantly for the meat
balls of raw burger he gobbled
fast as we could plop them into the pink
diamond-shaped hopper he offered as a target,
his head cocked back, his beak hinged open wide
to the neighborhood of kids waiting their turn,
writhing in hysterics
in the grass. Everything shiny caught Jack's eye,
to the chagrin of my father—maniacal,
bad back-yard mechanic
who valued his tools like doubloons,

who raged beneath the Buick,
his black-greased gorilla hand
blindly slapping for a socket long gone.

Mother loved that cockamamie bird
because he took her back to childhood,
to another pet crow who chanted "Hell-*low*
Al-**bert**!—her brother's name—Al-**bert**!
through the same neighborhood. I crowed for months
to Jack cocking his leathery black
hole-in-the-head-for-an-ear
toward my phonics, 'til the words took hold
in *his* bird brain: "Hell-*low*, **Paul**! Hell-*low*, **Paul**!"
he mimicked all day long from the deck
where he limped like Blackbeard, one leg
wrapped in a popsicle-stick splint
after the family dog, taking all
the constant talk and guano
in his food dish he could take, snapped.

"Hell-*low*, **Paul**!" Jack squawked
until the day he disappeared. But not before he ran
the umpteenth pair of Mrs. Lupino's nylons,
her ankles welted raw. "Hell-*low*, **Paul**!
How-she-go-*een*! How-she-go-*een*!"
And though he added to his raspy repertoire,
he never did say where he cached
Dad's 36-piece Craftsman socket set—
like words, one sunlit glimmer at a time.

HiCaw

Talking crow bucks wind
Chortles "***Paul!***" with mouth full "***Paul!***"
Beaked night gleams my name

For My Mother, Delia, Auntie Alma,
Uncle Albert, and Grandpa Romano

THE WHALE IN MY WALLET

We're talking humpbacks, not greenbacks,
but I'm still sitting fat
packing only his flukes—biggest fingerprints
you ever saw high-fiving me
or, should I say "two-hi-ing" me out of the gray
Atlantic—Sable Island to Stellwagen Bank
to New York Bight—or maybe out of the blue
Caribbean, off Puerto Rico, off Haiti,
off the Grenadines. He moves around a bit,
this ubiquitous humpback, this quasi-
Quasimodo, I suppose, of his pod,
after some three-story-tall titanic
propeller or snaggle-toothed denizen
out of Davy Jones's Locker
chewed his dorsal fin off his back, and left him
with his anatomical namesake—you guessed it—
Stub! Not Neptune, Rigadoon, Tom Cruise, Sing-A-Tune,
not even peg-legged Blackbeard or Captain Hook,
but just plain old monosyllabic-ugly, *Stub*,
like the nickname of a Polish-Italian hit man,
Stub Podgurski, *Stub* Lagunowski, *Stub* Mitolio—
monikers from my hometown phone book! *Stub*, like Bub
or rub-a-dub-dub, like grub, or tub-o-lard butt,
but beauty, we know, is only blubber-deep,
and even if Charlie-the-talking-tuna *were* picked
by Starkist, he'd still be just a fish!

Stub, on the other fin, is tops,
to paraphrase his adoption papers,
"...at playing tag and torpedo
with the whale-watching boats." It's *Stub*!—
the humpback ham-atola! The leviathan
lampooner! The coxswain lob-tailing, stand-up comic
of the deep—the salt-water Sinbad, Don Rickles,
Rodney Dangerfield and breaching John Belushi

reincarnated! All roly-polied into one! No—wait!
It's the B. B. King of the Barnacle-Blues! You bet,
me buckos, this galley-hound Elvis-the-Pelvis, this Sinatra-
of-the-sea can sing! We're talking ocean virtuoso,
not babbling Brooks, and certainly not *Whalon*!
We're talking *SEA*-W gods, The Hank-
meister, The Hag, and, yes, Johnny The-Man-In-Black
Cash, all of whom drank like nuns
next to Stub. We're talking M. C. (Marine-Cool) Hammer-
The-Humpback-Jammer, who, rumor has it,
raps in rhymed iambs. My main man,
Stub, the sea-*leb* of all sea-*levs,*
and let's *see* Michael Jackson moonwalk water!
Which is why I carry this deep-sounder,
page-to-glassined-page, baleen-face-to-bearded-face
with old J. C.—talk about your Heavies! Talk about
your family-at-*large*! Talk about your big bang
and the big splash I make
with strangers when I point to Stub and say
        "DAT SA MA BOY!"

For Mary Kathleen "Kitty" Collins

ZEKE ZARZYSKI

I. EIGHTY-SIXED

Zeke, hung over, with me and Liz in tow,
plows his way into a faux-fern-bar bistro
arf-arfing his favorite cow dog yarn about the dude
who strolled into a Browning, Montana
Blackfeet watering hole
where Indian-cowboy rounders still ride
cayuses through the swinging saloon doors: "…so
this dandy, wearing arfing-arfing ("goofy-looking"),
fluorescent-orange Crocs
gets his foot stepped on by a horse
and when he whines to the proprietor
his threats to sue, the bulldogger-turned-
bar-owner snaps back, "who in the *arfing-
arfed* hell do you think you are
coming in here *afoot* in the first place!" Everyone—
well, most everyone—in the joint guffaws. Most
everyone buys Zeke shots of, yup,
"hair of the dog." Every breed of pooch-
hooch sizzles in the **ZZ**-monogrammed
water bowl on the bar
in front of the stool Zeke sits on
lapping, panting with Australian Shepherd
"sic-'em" glee. The tall tattooed bar maid
sports a smirking prairie dog
perched between her animated mounds of cleavage
inches from Zeke's blue eye
as she strokes Zekes's pink belly right above
his you-know-what. Life
has never been this rousing for a cow hound
in town, *until*, that is, the no-doubt jealous,
sawed-off, Chihuahua-faced manager,
decries Zeke's kind—"a shedding,
slobbering, crotch-nosing, womanizing

cur"—*unwelcomed*! Zeke and I,
along with poor mortified Liz, and most
every male patron feeling *he'd* been singled out,
get up to leave. Zeke, lifting his leg
on the "Tonight's Specials"
chalkboard easel on his way out the door,
snarls, "Considering the arf-arf ("horse-poop")
arf-arfing ("hoof-paring") canine cuisine
you serve, us Aussie dogs, especially, ought
to be arfing (censored) catered to here
with open dewclaws!" Designated driver Zeke,
drooling, pulls over three times on our way home
when I caution him that I'm about to toss
my cookies. I should know by now
never, *ever*, to say "cee-oh-oh-kay-eye-ee"
when Zeke's behind the wheel.

II. BECKONS HIS MASTER TO FETCH

Zeke cherishes his bucketful of blue
racquetballs, like his *very* best one
that rolled, slow motion, down a gopher hole—
the 60-foot putt, replay after replay
after replay, the only footage
on the JumboTron screen of his canine
mind. I know all too well
how he feels. I also have lost friends,
family, youth, wealth, good looks,
down similar deep dark holes
into the underworld unknown—not
a rubber ball's bouncing prayer
in melting hell of ever retrieving
what was once so dear to me. Therefore,
on this day-of-no-rest-for-the-dogged-

Polish-Italian-Good-Samaritan—
our neighbors all *digging their* just rewards
in church—what precise timing,
I decide, to schlep pick-axe, spade,
pry bar, dynamite (if Liz
has not squandered it all to bust open
her garden plot in this god-forsaken
landscape of hardscrabble clay)
into the pickup box with Zeke, who,
panting, pacing, can't wait to show me
which one of the countless gopher
holes pocking his stomping grounds
swallowed his beloved ball. Long past
communion and Sunday brunch,
I, both hands blistered, bleeding, with Zeke,
both front paw pads raw from spelling me
between boulder extractions,
finally spy the blue-eyed
Cyclops peering up at us from somewhere
near Shanghai, way down slope
east of Greece. Rattlesnakes, black widows,
brown recluses be damned, I reach shoulder-deep
into the shaft and, inch-by-gingerly-finger-tipped-inch, roll
ol' blue toward the surface, with Zeke
the whole while licking my one ear
not cookie-cuttered into the dirt—as though
something really, really, *really* critical
has been lost in *that* hole, as well.

III. GRIDIRON PORN STAR

Zeke, sprawled on the avocado-green
living room shag, twitches, wuffs, yelps,
yips in action-motion-picture-show
dreams at the Canine Stardust Drive-In
Theater. He relives the day's ball
fetchings, snake/cat/jackrabbit sightings,
horse wranglings and, it being football season,

the one-on-one drill we practice together
when Zeke's TV instinct kicks-in at kick-off
to the cadences of the game or better
yet when I catapult off the couch
shouting Zeke's favorite word "Go. Go!
Go-**GO-GO!** during a Green Bay
Packer dash for the end zone. Zeke,
springing into his tail-stub-wagging,
blue-eyed-wide, four-point stance,
sets (yes, it's "sets" here, *not* "sits") as I,
across the room, bark out
the long count—Hut-One! *Food*-Ball! Hut-Two!
Who's There! Horse Cookie! Hut-Three! *Go* Pee-Pee! *Go*
Chicago Bear!* *Go* NaNa-NuNu!** Cat! Cat!
Hut-*Hut*!—hiking the pigskin up tight
into the crook of my arm as I stutter-
step toward open-field
tackler, Zeke. "Wrapping me up,"
his front paws clamped around my thigh
while I slo-mo-tumble into a lovable heap
right in front of the LG HD screen, Zeke,
hump-hump-humping my leg, *totally*
ignores referee Liz, in hysterics,
blowing the dog whistle,
throwing the yellow dishtowel flag,
announcing to the television
crowd booing her call,
"personal (*extremely* personal)
foul—15-yard penalty for excessive
humper-doodling
way, *way* too long after the play!"

To Zeke's "Uncle Ricky" Helms, and in Memory of Rin Tin
Tin, Bullet the Wonder Dog, Old Shep, Wolfie, and Lassie

*go Poo-Poo
**go Beddy-Bye

49

A LESSON IN ANIMAL ZEN

"Animals make us Human."
Temple Grandin

Built for full-grown cattle, the alley-
way to the squeeze chute is far
more than just a Hereford hair
too wide for the five-seven-ten head
of calves not at all funneling
smoothly into single file,
doing their best worst
impersonation of duodenal colic, gall-
stone pile-up in the bile duct,
a saber-toothed tiger with a woolly
mammoth hairball. They clog, clot,
curdle, coagulate, contort, leap-
frog, one-eighty, you-name-it,
turning what we reckoned
would be a cakewalk
job into utter chaos, into just another
ranch-day snafu. We therefore are
forced to revisit our mission
statement, to put the Yosemite Sam
"WHOA!"on the bug-eyed little varmints,
to back-off, bring them solo,
temper our methods of beckoning—no
further coaxing with splintered rails,
broken fence posts, snapped-off-
an-inch-above-the-thumb
cattle prods, no four-letter words
strung together into the mother of all
polysyllabic cussing, no
umpteen hocks poked out between the slats on both sides
of the alleyway looking from above
like some weird hybrid
Petri dish cross between *Megalosaurus*
and a polliwog orgy. We place ourselves,

instead, in their diminutive hooflets,
institute the peace-n-love plan
to "pacifying," rather than "punching,"
cattle. We even own up to
our innermost bovine sides, yield
to the yin and yang
of our metaphysical hindrance, tone
down our yips, whistles, clicks,
which, animal husbandry science aside,
simply *is* akin to talking baby talk
to the "little dogies," getting along now—
"whoop-ee-ti-yi-o"
just like in the ol' cowboy song!—
without imbroglio bellow or bawl. Working
its literal "out of the *blue*,"
soothing smooth way
through the stirrup-boned alleys
of our middle ears, is the subliminal
wisdom children teach
their teachers during recess—swing-set
playgrounds from our childhood past
echoing this clamor, this steady
clanking cadence of squeeze chute steel.

For Curt, Carol, and Jess Stewart

PHOTO FINISH

Because a horse cannot see its own nose,
the bell mare stares at herself
mesmerized in the mirrored glass
vet clinic door—fixates so firmly
she's distracted from her chronic pain,
her herd-bound angst, her equine
gender's, shall we say, "testiness"? Deaf
to the duct tape's reptilian hiss
ripping off the roll—the vet
figure-eighting both front Styrofoam-padded hooves—
Cody, lulled by a million cc's curiosity,
balances passively on three legs
until, almost one wing beat too soon, a finch,
flitting through her reflection, snaps
her out of her hip-cocked hypnotic trance back to
her fractious, pawing, snorting self
hell-bent to load up and haul home.
                                    Trailer
rocking a Richter-scale 6.8 on its hitch,
the Ford's flopping rearview tilts
just enough to force me to ponder,
glimpsing right, my own profile,
though, with one eye closed, *I can see*
purt-near around the prow of the nose
I've preferred all my life not
to regard too closely.
                        Pushing fifty now,
I take my cues from wise old Cody,
thrice her twenty-five years. I decide this,
indeed, is a Triple Crown nose, a nose
with "run for the roses" written all over it—thick
antithesis of *aquiline*, or even *equine*,
yet still reaching far enough beyond my hat brim
to absorb healthy photonic doses of solar vitamin D,
to make each and every oxygen molecule

feel especially welcomed. It's that kind
of in-with-the-good, out-with-the-bad
nose that discerns, three blocks off,
fine cuisine from rancid grease,
alluring pheromones from cheap perfume,
music from boom box blare—our ears, admit it,
the worst of the five-senses-slackers
since the eyes accepted polyester.
                                Nostrils flared,
rhinoplasty be damned, this is *thee* nose
for poetry, a prosodic nose, a nose that will
bulldog and bulldoze its way
to the flashbulb finish line of life
where that un-retouched snapshot will prove
aerodynamically-challenged me
"The Winner."

For GT (Gary Thompson) who, for good
reason, calls me "Horse."

COWBOYS & INDIANS

FRONTIER ANESTHESIA (a Jingle)

"When men were men and whiskey was bourbon,"
When "doc" was the doctor and "sawbones," the surgeon,
A bottle of Bulleit is what they'd be servin'
Each time they extracted some lead from your person—
And though you can bet it hurt quite a lot,
When the Bourbon's this good, you can't wait to get shot!

When my father does not ride in on time
for supper, I track him down,
find him wounded, fevered,
slumped on his big hairy Ernest
Borgnine forearms over his work bench
in the shop across the yard. Quivering,
sweat soaked through both his shirts,
he twists and torques
with needle-nose pliers in one fist
treble hooks of a Heddon Torpedo
run deep into the forefinger
of the other, bleeding
like a northern pike
gaffed through the gills.
                        He is the victim
of television westerns we watched
together every Saturday—Hoppy,
Widmark, Cooper, Fonda, Mix,
as cowboy or cavalry scout
in that patented scene where he
torturously forces
the Arapaho, Comanche, Chiricahua, Shoshoni,
Sioux arrow he's been skewered by
all the way through his shoulder, snaps
the point off and then—to melodramatic

orchestral crescendo—pulls the slick
shaft back through
cleanly.
       Clearly, my pop has forgotten how
they'd all pass out cold, more than
a little to do, perhaps, with redeye
gizzard juice they'd guzzle,
save for that last antiseptic splash
spilled into the wound,
not to mention the ever-present
partner or sidekick, ever-ready
to cauterize—Bowie knife
agleam in the campfire's writhing
flame, in the moonlight's blaze. "**Dad!**
I scream in lieu of puking,
"Who in the heck do you think you are? Wild Bill
Polack?"
       The surgeon, shaking
his noggin in Doc-Adams-of-Gunsmoke disgust,
works a fishing-leader-like, looped
wire gizmo to back the barbs
my father drove bone-deep
eventually out. "Lucky for us, hey Dad,"
I quip, driving home from Emergency—"lucky
they didn't pack extractors like that
back in the old West?" He grins
and I, together with him
again in front of our 1950's Zenith TV,
gaze at the legendary
reflected in the windshield—big screen
cowboy hero he will always be.

For Anne and Richard Widmark

WOODCHUCK LOVE

The summer after my father faded
into life's final hibernation, after
I consecrated with his gray remains
the sturdiest sugar maples, birch,
black ash and oaks in his woodlot,
Woody the Woodchuck—from god-
of-the-cuddly-far-out-varmints
only knows where—dropped in
unannounced at 505 Poplar, Mom and Dad's
first and only home. Woody
has crashed here for three summers—his digs
(and I do mean *digs*) beneath Dad's tool shed,
beneath Dad's woodpile, alongside
Dad's garden, grown over now
so sadly with dandelions. Woody
has become the talk of the neighborhood,
May through August, as he grows more
roly-poly with each season's green
grass he mows not quite as evenly
as Dad's John Deere. When not dining,
Woody sprawls, half under, half out,
of the tool shed's stoop. Flattened
into the cool humus, he breathes less
conspicuously than a Zen master
meditating on the meaning of fur-
bearing life. Woody peers due north
toward the cattywampus wood
pile's sink-holed tiers—thanks to the shafts

Woody's dug with Dad's knack
for mining iron ore deep in the Cary
decades back. As went Dad, so goes
Woody—*not* adored by all. I, therefore,
am forced to implore the neighbors
not to rat Woody out to the DNR*
for his vagrant ways, for his late-night-snack
cravings for tender lettuce and flower petals
in their gardens and yards. Woody
(as surely you must savvy by now) *is* my dad
reincarnated. Which, understandably, is
why his chip-off-the-old-woodchuck-block
son is so intent on having a heart-to-heart
with him. Why I've placed Dad's hand-
crafted oak bench beside his lounging
spot beneath the tool shed's stoop
where he lies in the July shade
during the siesta heat of the day. I sit
there stump-still, a frosty can of Pabst
Blue Ribbon between us in the grass
until, inch-by-cautious-curious-woodchuck-inch,
he appears, as if answering the imaginary
knock of kinfolk at his screen door—
his dark eyes alive with what I fathom,
in my most monkish mulling, as woodchuck
love. Not, mind you, to be confused
with that ridiculous Captain & Tennille ditty
"Muskrat Love," but rather, far more

ethereal, woodchuck love, which
(and I know you're with me on this)
is akin to those sentimentalities that we,
the supposed chosen, soul-bearing mammals
stake sole claim to? Okay, I'll admit
here in indelible poetic ink
that, at first, I *did* talk baby talk
to Woody. Wising up,
however—reminded by his scowl
that he is in-fact my dad, Leonard-
The-Gruff—I soon changed my tune
and tone of voice. Even as Dad lay dying,
as helpless as a newborn in the arms
of hospice nurses, I did not talk baby talk
to him. I have also resisted thus far
the most obvious question: so, dear old Dad,
just how much wood *does* a woodchuck
chuck when a woodchuck does
chuck wood? I mean, what if
our good neighbor, Beverly Lombardo, hears
us through her screen door and,
instead of questioning her own
damn sanity, instead of suspecting her
latest medley of meds, she turns
us in to Animal Control? Me and Woody,
(I mean Dad) *would* be chucking wood
at the screw-loose calaboose, the bat-shit
chateau of the Badger State—the cheesehead-

lobotomy lodge on Lake Winnebago! I pop the top
on our umpteenth PBR, place it
near Woody's door. The tear-stained
note plastered to the foaming can
reads, "Dearest Dad—From here on out,
we best keep it to a whisper. Your woodchuck-
loving, loving-woodchuck son, Paul."

For Beverly, with love

*Department of Natural Resources

They Travel In Twos

DRINKING WITH MISTER MINK

A yard sale one-of-a-kinder, stuffed
likely by a master cannabis gardener
turned amateur taxidermist
after the harvest, Mr. Mink,
fastened to a burled root,
perches on his haunches
like a dog begging, his front legs
poised precisely enough apart to grip
the hefty shot glass
I slide between his paws. Mr. Mink—
his sentimental little head tilted
left with expectation, his right eye
like a window into a soul bursting with thirst—
implores that I pour him another,
and another, and…well…no way
could I *ever* allow such a fellow-
forlorn animal-traveler
to drink alone, now, could I?
                              Could *you* have
said "I'll pass, ma'am" to the animated
woman asking a pittance for such
a prized man-cave find
at her "My Husband Became A Monk
So I'm Selling All His Dumb Stuff,
Thank You God Sale?" And, no, damn it,
I have not yet gotten besotted enough
to check, so don't bother asking. He's *Mister*
Mink, okay? Period. Case closed.
                              Thusly,
here we sit, the old ermine-whisperer,
Zarzyski, raising a late-night nip
with Mr. Mink, our glasses clinking
to *Na zdrowie! Salute! Prosit! Skoal!
Sláinte!*—the latter, *Sláinte!*,
distinctly familiar to Mr. Mink, in sync,

62

I think, with his taste for Jameson,
Tullamore Dew, and one Irish hooch
he seems most approving of,
Writers' Tears. Speaking of which, at first
when I'd read to Mr. Mink my latest
poetic *chef-d'oeuvre*—yes, that is,
indeed, French, for "masterpiece"—
his palpable silence, as if to imply
"you surely ain't no William Butler Yeats,"
both hurt and perturbed me. Therefore,
I threatened to replace Mr. Mink
with a female Canadian cockatoo
named Poontang, who, I argued,
would at least hold up her colorful end
of the conversation. I'd teach Poontang,
I admonished Mr. Mink, to squawk her raucous
head-bobbing applause to my each
and every final-line epiphany:
"Effin'-A-tweety-bird! *Grrrr-ate* poem! *Grrrr-
ate* poem! Screw Yeats! *Grrrr-ate* poem!
Effin'-A-tweety, 'ey! '*eyyy!*"
                    Alarmed,
Mr. Mink now lauds each nuance
of my prosody, thanks in no small part
to the art of ventriloquism. I'm relieved—
it being just a little tricky these days
smuggling a loquacious, potty-mouthed
cockatoo through Canadian Customs: "Effin'-
A-tweety-bird! Hide the reefer! Dudley Do-Right!
Hide the reefer, '*eyyy!*"
                    Mr. Mink is *not* high,
as you might surmise by now,
on the mere thought of a chatty cockatoo
named Poontang, *nor*, in general,

on Canadians, who he faults
for the fur trade. "Why else
would they call it a mink stole, if not
for the fact that those pesky Canucks *stole* it
off the backs of my kinfolk," I hear him
mulling it over out loud. Mr. Mink,
so comfortable in his own skin,
is not one bit shy about touting META
(Mink for the Ethical Treatment of Animals)
when tipping a few among his simpatico
fur-bearing friends. And, therewith,
we drink my word reservoirs dry,
our final toast of the night
"to silence," after which, I, turning in,
feel comforted in the knowing
that, come morning, Mr. Mink will be there
for me, right where I left him, dead-
center on our kitchen table,
his shot glass still half full, the lucky stiff.

For David Wilkie, the Only Canuck Musician to Ever
Drink Mister Mink under the Table

FLAT CRICK'S MAD GOURMET POET AND HIS FISHING FANATIC NEIGHBOR HOLD THE FIRST-EVER POLECATTING DERBY

When noxious fumes put the kibosh on our *Bon Appétit*
Christmas feast—our eyes instead of mouths
watering into platefuls of spiced cognac yams,
wild virgin gosling, and chestnut dressing—I retched
beyond the galactic brink of sanity
into the black hole of madness. From mothballs
by the bucketful, to garlands of garlic,
to Rolling Stones' "Sympathy for the Devil"
full-volume for hours, to boiling
concoctions of Starbucks French Roast, balsamic
vinegar, and Brown Mule Chewing Tobacco, I tried
every folk gimmick to peacefully eighty-six the passel
of polecats playing grab-ass, night and day,
under the house. I tracked them with an ear
pressed flat against the floor, my Colt .45
cocked and chattering
over ripples of blistered linoleum as I stroked—
a wind-up toy gone berserk. I bounced,
"fa-la-la-la-la-la," off the wall and down the hall
decked with hopeless aromatic boughs of holly
until I came red nose to red nose with the Homelite
chainsaw, like a brainstorm, under the tree
right next to the Cuisinart electric juicer.
To the million-decibel whine, exhaust seeped
through foundation cracks, streaks of purple
chain oil, like flogging welts,
crisscrossed the sheet-rocked walls,
and sawdust fallout lemon-peppered our 8-course meal.
My *former* fiancée, hoping someone could talk me down,
phoned the neighbor—not knowing he'd join
any fracas that smacked of fishing. We buzzed
a dozen holes just square enough to fit
our heads between the joists. "Pepé?

Pepé Le *Pewww*? Where are *youuu*?" we crooned
until what we *thought* were their frontal eyes shining
puckered from the black
fumarole to their polecat château
beneath my kitchen table. That *did* it. We set traps
chained to long cottonwood limbs,
ran a hose from the sink through the floor—
whetted our fishing fancies,
flushed the interlopers out—and trolled
for polecats. You might say, we caught our limit
but still got skunked, showed no mercy,
took no prisoners, granted no parole, not one
catch-and-release penchant from the hard-hearted
mad poet and his coup de grâce henchman. We were smitten,
you might say, with holiday spirit nonetheless,
rosier than jolly ol' Saint Nick,
as we, a mile apart at our bachelor abodes,
soaked beneath lemon
flotillas in our matching claw-footed bathtubs
flanked by gallon-can Heinz convoys,
boxes of baking soda, and sidekick
fifths of Smirnoff vodka—jingle, jingle,
ice cube jingle, all the Bloody Mary way
to the Flat Crick Lonely Hearts Polecatters Club
First Annual New Year's Eve Pot-luck Mixer. Yup,
just the fuming-drunk two of us, drunker
than a you-know-déjà-vu-what,
but still not blotto enough
to stomach the reeking Beaujolais bouquet,
the fetor of *pâté de foie gras*, the noxious
Munster with truffles stench—let alone
stand downwind from the Roma tomato
aftershave of juiced-up one another.

For Curt Stewart

ZARZYSKI GOES DAFFY WITH ZUPAN ON THE LAST DAY OF QUACKER SEASON

"The stormy road home is the best road home
for the man who would bring back ducks."
Gordon MacQuarrie
Stories of the Old Duck Hunters

"…Partner, I don't give a gander's ass,
so don't ask me again what
the *poor* folks are up to today. All I know,
it's the eighth of January, worst
rawboned blizzard in years—minus
visibility, drifts taller than the abominable
snowman hisself, colder than a frozen turd
in a dead polar bear—and the *poor*,
no-doubt, are somewhere cozy as toast,
with the ducks, sittin' one *hell*uvalot
farther south and flusher than us."

"*But Partner,*" he pleads, "grit your teeth,
hang tough, we'll jump them,
you'll see—full-plumage drakes—
those late flights, so fat on Canadian grain
they quack in French and crap whole-wheat
biscuits on the wing. Look for steam,
that warm-water slough—*steam!*—
then we'll stalk, crawl, burrow through
these cornices for cover, and *badda-boom,*
hit 'em with our ol' ZZ&Z
double zed-men green-weenie
number 5 magnum surprise!"

"*Don't fret*," he rants on, "about icicles
hanging out our barrels. They'll blow
clean on the first barrage. And the truck?
We'll spot her, *no sweat*, once we find the road.
Chain up all four, use our bag limit
for ballast in the tail end—*backtrack*
that's all! Just *imagine* the sky,"
he raves, "*black* with mallards
snafued against this wind—snowflakes,
lead shot, and feathers *bursting*
like fireworks! Imagine the *fusillade*!
The *volley*! The *salvo*! Imagine
The Fourth of July!"

Imagine *this*, folks: two rare birds
on the brink of extinction,
on snowshoes, *on* display
in some taxidermist's shop window—
our pump-guns shouldered, frost-bitten
cheeks wedged into the stocks, fingertips
frozen, mid-squeeze, to the triggers—
Diehard Zupan and Tag-Along Zarzyski
taking serious bead through the glass
eyes of the BB-brained, Loony-Tuned
last-dayer. *That's all Folks!*

For Kim

68

ESCORTING GRAMMY TO THE POTLUCK ROCKY MOUNTAIN OYSTER FEED AT BOWMAN'S CORNER—A LOVE POEM

Lean Ray Krone bellers through a fat cumulus
cloud of Rum-Soaked Wagonmaster Conestoga
Stogie smoke he blows across the room,
"They travel in twos, so better eat them even
boys, or kiss good luck good-bye for good."

Tonight the calf nuts, beer-batter-dipped
by the hundreds, come heaped
and steaming on 2-by-3-foot trays
from the kitchen—deep-fat fryers
crackling like irons searing hide.

And each family, ranching Augusta
Flat Crick country, brings its own brand
of sourdough hardrolls, beans, gelatins,
slaws and sauces, custard, and mincemeat
pies to partner-up to the main chuck.

At the bar, a puncher grabs a cow-
poxed handful—7 of the little buggers—
feeding them like pistachios
from palm to pinch fingers to flick-
of-the-wrist toss on target.

Grammy, a spring filly at 86, sips
a whiskey-ditch in one hand, scoops
the crispy nuggets to her platter
with the other, forks a couple
and goes on talking Hereford bulls.

And me, a real greenhorn to this cowboy
Caviar—I take to them like a pup
to a hoof paring, a porky
to a lathered saddle, a packrat
to a snoosebox filled with silver rivets.

I skip the trimmings, save every cubic inch
of plate and paunch for these kernels,
tender nubbins I chew and chew 'til the last
pair, left for luck, nuzzle on the tray
like a skylined brace of round bales.

A cattleland Saturday grand time with Grammy
is chowing down on prairie pecans, then driving
the dark-as-the-inside-of-a-cow grangehall
trail home to dream heifer-fat, bull-necked
happy dreams all night long in my Sunday boots.

For Ethel "Grammy" Bean

DEER HEART (AND GENTLE PEOPLE)

"A *must* cuisine for the country music purist,"
I tell my pal, Quinton Mush-Heart Duval, "the Q'ster,"
wincing as I rinse the mule deer's ticker in the sink—
filling and spilling the pinkish liquid
from the ruby-red goblet of life until, *oops,*
a huge black leech of coagulated blood
plops, then slithers down the drain. I slip
my fingers into the heart, and holding it upside down,
place it like a puppet close to Q's face
and mimic for him my most alien-eating monotoned
"consume large quantities"
ventricular Conehead ventriloquism.

We have been "drinking the heart right out
of a fine spring afternoon," to quote
the heart-and-soul prose of Missoula's one-and-only
Jim Heart-Throb Crumley. To graduate students
of serious lit-tra-chewer and C-W tunes, it's easy to say
"our crimson couch with heartache trembles
like Patsy Cline's tender, sweet lips"
when the stereo plays her, full-volume,
singing (reader must croon along)
"...and I'm cra-   vin'
                zee for lu-   you-oooo."
                        u-

It is not the onions I blindly dice by heart
that make us cry into our Buckhorn beer,
and by now Q is heartily watching me
as we prattle heart-to-heart the art of poetry—
nothing quite like *ars poetica* to tug
the ol' heartstrings as I snip
those elastic atrial ligaments, and meticulously
skive away the hard outer black-veined fat
but then, having a quick change of heart, I opt

to cube rather than stuff, and have
the heart searing in the pan, lickety-split,
or shall we say, "in a heartbeat?" Truth is
(cross my heart and hope to die)
I braise it in bacon drippings, splash in
copious glug-glug-glugs of grad-student Beaujolais,
eight shakes of Worcestershire, soy, and Pickapper sauce,
add a skosh of Liquid Smoke, Pound's Cantos,
grated ginger root, umpteen garlic gloves,
purple onion, jalapeño, and pink-bottom stump
mushrooms to my heart's content.

Belting out a slow-tempo'd
"take these chains from my heart and set me free,"
I ladle it wholeheartedly over polenta
while Q nasals the refrain to "heartaches
by the dozen," crudely burps
and murmurs something chicken-hearted
about his killer heartburn
kiboshing his appetite. He knows my heart is set
on this mellifluent repast for two. He knows
I'll be broken-hearted if he doesn't show
at least a little heart, so he digs in
like a finicky kid eating bony fish,
both of us by now walkin' the honky-tonkin'
heartsick blues beat of life with Hank pourin'
His heart into a little ol' tune
that jerks the teardropped hearts
right out of me and Q when He croons,
        eat-
" you're   in'   we'll
       hearrrt—   tell on
              youuu."

In Memory of Quinton—In tribute to his posthumous
book of, you bet, hearty *poetry,* Like Hay.

ZARZYSKI STOMACHS THE OXFORD SPECIAL WITH ZIMMER AT THE OX BAR & GRILL

Donning his bronc-stomper black hat, cockeyed
the morning after reading range rhymes
in Montana, Zimmer swears out loud
his belly's tough as whang leather,
reckons his grease count's a skosh low,
and it behooves us, here in cattleland,
to brunch on cow—no quiche,
no veggie omelet or hen-fruit Benedict
when Zimmer's craving beeve, a hoof-n-horn
dogie-puncher dose of B-12
to prod toward procreation
two brain cells the whiskey failed to pickle.

Zarzyski thinks Zimmer figures
rare steak and eggs-a-pair
'til he catches Zimmer's pupils, ruminating
behind the stained menu—his devious gleam.
Zimmer has brains on the mind.

Zimmer has brains on his mind
and Zarzyski knows too well the Zimmer dictum:
"What suits one P. Z. damned straight tickles
another P. Z. plum pink." Sure as shit
and shootin', like a gunslinger
demanding redeye, crusty-throated Zimmer hollers,
"Bring us hombres brains and eggs!"
And the waitress relays Zimmer's whimsy
to a fry cook big enough to eat hay
and dirty-up the floor. In short-order lingo
she yells, "These boys *need 'em*, Sam—
these Z-boys *need 'em* real awful bad."

For Paul Zimmer—aka P. Z. [1], *C.C. (Carne Cabesa)* [11]

RED SHUTTLEWORTH'S BIRTHDAY, BASEBALL, BOILERMAKER BARDS BOMBASTIC, AND THE HORRIBLE, BUT VICTORIOUS, MORNING AFTER

His lower lip squeegees the Guinness
foam from his Johnny Ringo mustache
shining silver in the kitchen
light where we drink
the post-poetry-reading polite applause
out of our lives. Cleansing
our palates with one long last pull each
off a fifth of Bushmills, Red preaches
The Durham Bulls Gospel
according to Dirty Al Gallagher
skippering the club
in Red's bullpen catcher heyday. Red,
the only poet on curveball earth
to have caught *The Van Meter Heater*,
demonstrates—sofa as backstop,
housecat curled asleep at home plate—
the knuckler, the change-up, the cutter,
sinker, splitty, slider, screwball, plus
a dozen other lollapaloozas
I am beautifully too boozed-up
ever to remember. Quaffing the heavenly
guts out of the sanctimonious Moses
Lake night, we hoist our glasses
with swagger to Hank and Haggard
amped-up on the family boom box—to Willie,
Waylon, Cash, Van Zandt,
Lucinda-the-poet's-daughter-Williams,
Tom Russell and Bob Dylan, lusty

song lyrics honky-tonkin' us deeper
into testosterone nirvana. We talk tough
buckers and long-ball-hitters—Ruth to Moonshine,
DiMaggio to Rodeo Rose, Gehrig, Maris,
Aaron, Williams, Mays...The Mick
to Midnight. When Red reads me a pistol
about his slugger son, Luke Appling Junior,
sleeping with a coyote, we howl to the Irish
wolfhound, Piper, yodeling to Dave Alvin
blues, to the last lonesome October fly stirring
at sunrise from an east sill. Our porthole
on the poetry peep show we peer into
this instant, features a juicy *gusano*
beckoning from the Davy Jones locker
bottom of a half-full bottle
of rotgut *mezcal*. Lucky for us, today
is not *quite* that day good enough
to die on, in the wake of
pitching steely-eyed God
high and inside.

For Kate, Ciara, Jessi, Maura,
Luke, and What's Left of Red

The Guns Of Provolone

ZARZYSKI, NOT EXACTLY WILD BILL HICKOK

Forty-seven times my shotgun thundered,
a downpour of BBs riddles the sloughs,
as I wade knee-deep in Winchester hulls
red as rose hips and my cheeks.
Smokey, my retriever, pants
at my cursing and fist-shaking.
Forty-seven gossipy bluebills,
vanishing like words into a strong wind,
spread their tales from Saskatchewan
down the Mississippi flyway to New Orleans:
"That quack Zarzyski
couldn't pepper a duck
if the son-of-a-bitch was in the oven."

For Dave Books (a Quacker*jack Shot!)*

ATTACK OF THE BOX ELDER BUGS—*OR*, AS POET GREG KEELER WOULD PUT IT, "SOMEBODY BRING ME THE GODDAMNED BUG BOOK!"

Clinging to the sunny side of the house
crawling, I—wired
to one hundred feet of florescent orange extension cord
dangling from my crippled stepladder—
vacuum the outside south wall, one more battle
lost to old Ma Nature. Eureka
canister vac handle in my purple grip,
a million and one bugs humming
the melody to that country-western hit
    "*please* release me, let me *go*
    for *I* don't love you anymore"
in perfect Insectivora-with-vibrato pitch,
I lean back to survey my work while wishing
my weapon of choice could morph
into a double-u double-u two flamethrower. Better
yet, "snow, you son-of-a-bitch, snow!" Be careful
for what you wish. It snows and not only snows,
but snows like spitfire against the south
side of the house osmotically sucking
the moribund bugs through the logs
and into my living room.
                        Permanent fixture now
sprawled like a glutton pet python
taking months to digest
a pot-bellied pig, the vacuum's bulging
canister has been painted
to complement the *funk,* not *feng, shui* décor—green
shag carpet to Naugahyde wagon wheel couch
to pot metal horse-clock collection
and Russell Chatham lithographs. Just
in the nick of time, I finally coil up
my *Boicea trivittata* sucker-upper into the hall closet
as our New Year's Eve guests arrive

already sozzled.
                    We guzzle two gallons of sangria
before someone points out the *pico de gallo*
is alive! Back-strokers splish-splash in the punch bowl!
The eight-foot-tall, dancing, green-
Styrofoam-saguaro-cactus-in-red-Santa-cap
Jose Cuervo liquor store display
(awarded by the clerks to a customer
of exceptional regularity) suddenly is
flocked orange and black!
                    In the midst of this
phantasmagoria—the herd of equine clocks striking
midnight—my winged-insect brain cells,
sporting festive dunce caps and spinning
tin fizgig noise-makers, grind
to the tune of "Auld Lang Syne." Pie-eyed
guests suddenly departed, I find
my pickled McZyski heartfelt self
partying hard with the lonesome
ghost of Robbie Burns,
a bottle of Loch Lomond
single malt Scotch, and a houseful
of six-legged drinking buds. On our knees, we,
bobbing and weaving around the brims
of our half-empty glasses, ululate in unison
"Should auld acquaintance be forgot…"
as only we crawling boxers,
eldering into the wee hours,
can belt the bugger out.

For Greggy

STUUFFF!

Braking for all sales—estate, yard,
auction, rummage, moving, garage—as well
as all thrifts—Saint Vinny's, Sally Ann's,
Goodwill, Open Hands—we stop
at nothing when it comes
to further stuffing our cars
already stuffed with *STUUFFF!* Good
stuff, gaudy stuff, fun stuff, stuff
so funky nobody even knows
what-in-thingamaBob-Fulton's-name-it-is
STUUFFF! Doohickey, tchotchke,
shoot-n-holler-Sherlock-Holmes,
are-you-blowing-menthol-smoke-
rings-up-my-royal-kazoo, gimcrack, whim-wham,
geegaw *STUUFFF!* You bet, we need it all,
every teensy-weensy bit of it, in order
to maximize space, to defy the *feng shui*
emptinesses of life, to define each day
by our finds, to shirk the minutest minimalist
floor-to-ceiling glimpse—basement,
stairwell, closets, crawl space, attic, halls,
heart, never stacked quite exactly deep
enough, always one more niche,
fissure, cubbyhole, cranny, crevice, nook,
one more nano-scintilla of our very being
still unfulfilled to the nth degree with—need
we say it yet again?—*STUUFFF!*

For Barbara McFarlane, and
in Memory of George Carlin—
His Hilarious Bit on **Stuufff!**

PORCH LIGHT WEB

All summer long the miller moths
crap their muddy runny watercolor crap
between brush strokes of pricey oil paintings
adorning my living room walls, goddamn
pointillism-tainting dust-bag vagabonds—
miles from the nearest trout stream,
from their eco-heroic food chain niche—
sons-a-bitches, anyway.
                              Stinking even worse
than rotten cantaloupe innards
when I splatter the flitting bastards
across the Zenith TV screen, my Reebok
Cross-trainer or current issue of *Bon Appétit*
hurled across the room, I finally learn
to arm myself instead with vacuum
cleaner equipped with fixed-bayonet
baseboard attachment, its thin slot
offering maximum long-distance
suction: thh-whip...thh-whip...
thh-whip...thh-whip-whip—*ohhh, baby,*
a fornicating double!
                      Bingo! Gotcha!
Voilà! I locate the nocturnal
Insectivorous vampireis menaces
sound asleep come sunup on the flip
side of every hanging work of art
that I oh-so-slowly tilt up
away from the wall just enough
to slide the nozzle within...thh-whip...
thh-whip...thh-whip-whip-whip...*ahhhh,* coitus
interruptus of a Lepidoptera
ménage à trois!
                  But the *real* thriller
begins at dusk, when I pop the top
on a frosty Tecate, pour myself a shot

of *reposado,* steer with my knees the La-Z-Boy
recliner over to the picture window, and slurp
with a vengeance the ocher refried
frijoles dripping from the butt-end of a burrito
as I flip the outdoor porch light switch
ON!
      Like a drive-in-theater teenager, I
cheer the villain in tonight's feature film,
The Return of the Ravenous Arachnid,
her kaleidoscopic eyes
incited by the sudden web-pluck
cornucopia of spitfire corn dogs, rocket ship
pigs-in-blankets, supersonic spring rolls,
apricot crepes in flight, aerodynamic
cannelloni, blintzes-on-the-wing—the mother of all
Godzilla spiders (oh yeah, you go, girl!)
at the all-she-can-roll-up-and-suck-dry
(thh-whip, thh-whip) miller moth buffet.

For Ruthie McRae, Carol Stewart, and Nancy Duval

OF MAN AND MOUSE *(with apologies to John Steinbeck)*

In their itsy-bitsy bucktoothed brainpans
my humble abode becomes Sun City, Arizona,
Cancun, Bermuda, Honolulu, a Carnival Cruise
rodent reunion on the Queen Gouda
to Velveetaville. September into June—
ten months winter, one month discombobulated
limbo, the other month damn pathetic
bobsledding in Montana—they shack-up
and taunt me and turn my temperance
of a Tibetan monk to slush.
                                        But…
who, I ask, lukewarm-blooded among us
can fault the beady-eyed
piebald freeloaders
for having gumption enough to come in
out of the cold? Whose bleeding heart can
not forgive their gnawing the felt
liners out of our packs, the fleece
off our saddle skirts—the stuffing, padding,
insulation out of everything stuffed,
padded, insulated with foam,
rubber, cotton, straw, solid rock…*ahhh
shucks*, and shit-oh-dear, to boot, sugar,
don't we all just love to mouse around,
to burrow-in and build our cozy nests
beneath our wool *blankies* and down
comforters come 40 below?
                                        But…
what *is* this furry squirming
groping back at my bare pinkies
pawing for the spare key

in the Dodge's jockey box's dark? What in *thee*...?
Where in *thee*...? Who in *thee* hiccupping hell
filled my right Nike's big toe
with only the minutest millet
from the sack of assorted bird fodder? My left
galosh with blue Decon pellets? My Handy Andy
hand shoes with dark chocolate
cookie-sprinkle look-alikes? "Dear
Mr. & Mrs. Meekless Deer Mice, I hereby declare war
upon your perpetually-pooping impudence—
your lethal hantavirus versus my *not*, so far,
victorious Victor trap lines, bar bait,
curare-dipped toothpick pits, glue boards,
bouncing Betty sharp cheddar, booby-trapped
brie and Trojan Horse gorgonzola. I'm bringing out
the Guns Of Provolone.
                    But...
be thee forewarned and be thee fraught
oh rodent brethren, with this foreboding—
to those left standing juggernaut-upright
go not the spoils but the toils:
hay thy lawn, bale thy knapweed,
shoe thy mule, doctor thy shoer,
shoo thee away Jehovah's Witnesses
milling about thy gate, black
helicopters hovering above thy rooftop,
alien spacecraft of bovine sawbones
mutilating by full-moon thy cattle, *all*
whilst thy eeny, meeny, miny, mo's
thy foreclosure notices, whilst thy hides
thy brand new Dodge diesel, thy brand new

John Deere, thy brand new old girlfriend
from thy repossessor—thy ex-wife—
who still expects thee to keep
thy sly lazy neighbor's cheap loose wire up
tight enough to keep thy sly lazy
neighbor's tight loose wife down. *And*—last
but not least—be-eth thee diligent
in thy spilling each morning of thy dollar-
purrrrr-bean-curd-serving
of Puss 'n Boots Vegan Cuisine
out of thy reptile-hide Tony Lama boots
back into thy pacifist pussy-
cat's personalized yellow bowl
marked **K I L L E R!**"

For Mick Vernon—in Memory of
Lisa, Who Loved to Laugh

CANTANKEROUS-N-RANK!

Cantankerous-n-rank,
So cantankerous-n-rank:
The cowboy walks the ranching plank,
Some days his heart so dark, so dank,
He ain't so suave, he ain't so swank,
He's just so blankety blankety blank
Guldang...cantankerous-n-rank—
He's cantankerous-n-rank!

Cantankerous-n-rank,
So cantankerous-n-rank:
His ev'ry twist and ev'ry yank
At rusty stubborn spikes ring-shanked
Some gunsel drove through hardwood plank
Just drives him all the more blank-blank
Guldang...cantankerous-n-rank—
He's cantankerous-n-rank!

Cantankerous-n-rank,
So cantankerous-n-rank:
With ev'ry pry and torque and crank,
No magic tools from Hardware Hank,
Just tractor patois far too frank,
Blankety blankety blank-blank-blank
Guldang...cantankerous-n-rank—
He's cantankerous-n-rank!

Cantankerous-n-rank,
So cantankerous-n-rank:
A hornet stings his horse's flank,
Which bucks him off a steep cutbank,
This waddlin' waddie's ego shrank,
As he limps home, so blankety-blank
Guldang...cantankerous-n-rank—
He's cantankerous-n-rank!

Cantankerous-n-rank,
So cantankerous-n-rank:
Who colandered his water tank?
Some trigger-happy hunter's prank?
He's seeing red—not hearing *thanks!*—
Spray-painting fence posts point-blank-blank
Guldang...cantankerous-n-rank—
He's cantankerous-n-rank!

Cantankerous-n-rank,
So cantankerous-n-rank:
Another warning from the bank
The morning after rotgut drank,
To his back-pocket checkbook sank
In arrears, he's blankety-blank
Guldang...cantankerous-n-rank—
He's cantankerous-n-rank!

Cantankerous-n-rank,
So cantankerous-n-rank:
His pride's been pummeled, paddled, spanked,
Not one *stinking* dollar, peso, franc
Of ranching profit has he stank,
No black, just **red**, *more* **RED**, blank-blank
Guldang...cantankerous-n-rank—
He's cantankerous-n-rank!

In sum, this ranch—this wench, this skank—
Has so rankled him with rancor,
With unromantic blank-blank angst,
As his tractor tranny clinks and clanks,
And all he eats is beans and franks,
His language rank, un-sacrosanct,
Sprouts bushy tails on all his Manx
Whose caterwauling loudly ranks
With his...blankety-*meow-meow*-blank
Guldang...cantankerous-n-rank!

For Wally and Clint McRae—Who've known
days like this ("Purt Near!") on
their beloved Rocker Six.

Hummocking Erumpent

AFTER SIPPING CHARDONNAY AND TALKING ART, TOSSIN' SHOTS POETICALLY AT DOC HOLLIDAY'S

Because Mike Sarich knows Carmen, the bartender,
who just so happens to love artists
inside and out, the same way
Sarich adores a '47 Harley
Knucklehead, tonight is our Lady Luck night
in Reno. Carmen's pouring Cuervo Gold
triples we could never spring for
on the fifty-simoleon honorariums we scored
reading our poems at the Bullet
Bob Blesse Black Rock Press
ink-slinger exhibit. Lit
under glass at Nevada's Museum
of Art, you might indeed glimpse
our civilized livers. But Doc Holliday's
neon, like an X-ray machine,
or insect zapper gone berserk,
flashes our true insides
in duplicate on the back bar
mirror. Janis, George, Jagger, Hendrix and The Hag
jam with Big Jim McCormick from the jukebox
that some yahoo more pie-eyed than we *artistes*
mistook for a quarter slot machine,
leaving us to cash-in on a jackpot
of eclectic selections. Valerie Serpa
jitterbugs—so hip in her big hair, wet vermillion
lipstick, and black fishnets,
she makes Monroe, all a-jiggle
in that paddleball scene from *The Misfits*,
look like Twiggy. Kirk Robertson,

feeling not exactly Gable-esque with mustache
mashed into the mahogany,
could give six cinematic, literati shits
about running mustangs or, for that matter,
running The Mustang Ranch, where,
as their motto once read, "Quality
Keeps Them Coming." Our wads shot,
our plastic damn near maxed,
Gailmarie Pahmeier, professor of creative writing
and head madam behind tonight's line-up,
stays just far enough south of sober to forget
to assign a designated driver. After all,
it is not, she knows, the bartender
Carmen, with her top-heavy tilt of the bottle,
but rather the arsenal of the artist
heart that will keep us going,
going, bullet-riddled gone,
down that long lawless literary street for more.

For the Old Reno Wild Bunch

YEVGENY ALEXANDROVICH YEVTUSHENKO: COWBOY POET

Purring growl of your Russian tongue makes love
to our women, suddenly erumpent and churning
erotic in public. Once they were sweet
cream butter melting to our Dutch oven touch
under slow even-burning coals of mesquite,
ash wood, piñon fires, but now they burn
hot in the flames of pitch wood pine—they sizzle,
smoke, scorch and ruin the cobbler
because of you, Yevgeny. The cold war over
does not mean the heat-seeking
Yevtushenko must strike, but you have
struck Elko like a Cossack Slim Pickins
forking the bomb to earth
in a switch-a-Rooskie take on *our* movie,
Dr. Strangelove. Stalking Siberian tiger,
you prowl the aisles, all perimeter seats
armed with women anxious to be anointed,
transfigured by one droplet of your love-
potion ambrosian spit. I *must* believe
they adore you merely because
you do not slobber them with Red Man
tobacco juice, with granules of Copenhagen snuff,
Brown Mule or Skoal. In your baggy corduroy britches
tucked inside reptile-hide boots
like some tinhorn Texan, you capriole from podium,
glide, prance, pivot, swoop, whirl, as if the room
effervesces with pinkish iridescent bubble-
bath bubbles shaped like Cupid hearts
popping to the hot soft guttural
touch of your phonics, of your skinny fingers
sculpting and scripting into sexy metaphor
the palpable air of our women's longing. You tempt them
away from our horse lather and leather pheromones

into the surrealistic—lure
them with your somniloquous lips. How dare you kiss
their thinnest skin, their rice-paper cheeks,
the silken backs of their hands gone limp
to your line's feminine, feline endings
gently penetrating their capillary
yearnings? How dare you
mesmerize us men into applauding
your pilferage? I have caught you *red*-handed,
Yevgeny! But, how do I indict a fellow knight-
errant from the ivory tower's round table
when so few of us make this crusade? The Cowboy
Coliseum exults and salutes you the *CZAR*-
zyski of Cossack Poetry, while boasting me
The Elko Yevtushenko. My Slavic compadre,
my comrade, my partner-in-rhyme, together
we extol what the soul knows
once solaced by poetry—it knows it wants more
poetry! But it is you who has exposed the sword
as impotent twig in your forest
of "Dwarf Birches." *You* who has led the brigadier
charge of words into battle for all those still
kept silent. "*Yes!* Yevgeny"—I shout "*Yes!*"
yes, the way to mankind's peace-filled helix
is through the chromosomal Y, its remnant
exiled within all men. Bring it on home,
Yevtushenko—bring us back to the mother world
where your poetry throws open the gates,
rolls and buries the barbed wire, bulldozes
the hormonal walls into rubble,
and hoists the white flag that allows us all,
unconditionally, to swoon for you.

For Sue Rosoff ("God bless your roast beef sandwich!")

MARTINI MCRAE & WHISKEY ZARZYSKI:
A BRACE OF BLACKJACK ACES

Three mush-hearted dealers changed careers
'cause they couldn't gut the cruelty and the guilt.
The pit boss's shot-glass-hard eyes broke to tears
watching, wrinkle-by-wrinkle, two cowpoke poker faces wilt.

Laughter in the rafters, the automated cameras convulsed
when walleyed Wally, holding 20, took a hit,
dealer showing 7. I heard his drumrolling pulse
above Mike Korn's cackling, caterwauling fit.

Me and Wally, we couldn't savvy what's the joke,
what's funny 'bout some palooka totin' off our loot
fast as stackin' bales—us goin' for broke
and him lathered through his pin-striped suit.

Shy on brain, but extra-*extra* long on sand and brawn,
we'd double-down on 3s or 5s and blow it.
But get pitched off, climb right back on—
"more chips! more drinks!" for the Marlboro bard & Polack poet.

We squandered all our gatherin's, includin' riggin' sack
and Rocker Six—wouldn't let us bet our poetry—
but then we sobered- and tallied-up, and lookin' back
we figures only winners drink all night "for free."

But poor McRae, still mutters something 'bout bad dreams,
asked why he's bruised and wearin' shades on rainy days.
He jolts in sleep, wife Ruth will vouch, and screams
"Hit me! Hit me! Hit me!" And she, wholeheartedly, obeys.

To All the Elko Gathering Cowboy Poets and Fans

THE ELKO ECDYSIAST—*OR*, WHAT HAPPENS IN ELKO AIN'T STAYING IN ELKO

"Darkness washed over The Dude—darker than
a black steer's tuchis on a moonless prairie night."
Sam Elliott
The Big Lebowski

Redefining "shock-n-awe," the stripper, on break,
takes a seat at our front-row, center-stage table
out of the bluest blue, making us believe
in life after death, patron saints of dumb luck,
"The Power of Positive Thinking," in mermaids,
guardian angels, sylphs and nymphs and good witches,
Sasquatch, the succubus, "Beauty and the Beast"—
in the "yellow brick road," itself! "You look like
nice mature men," she meows, to our drooling
catatonic cowboy-hatted senior trio,
her euphemistic "mature men" quip
blowing to bits what fragile minuscule egos
we feebly still cling to. I defend my youth-
fueled nubile-lewd eyes—"not so 'mature'
that I don't dig your stacked patent leather
bitchin' high-rise heels, sister,"
I purr back at her through the smoke
ring she smooches up and over
my noggin, as if to lasso,
like a cartoon caption, the raunchy,
pot-valiant, big-bad-wolfian
naughty thought hovering above me—"baa-a-a-a-a
babe, what voluptuously-groomed hooves,
what tutti-frutti cuticles, you have."
                        She launches
a perfumed leg up across my Wrangler-jeaned-
(forever-after-unlaundered) lap—her thigh-

high horizontally-striped silky stocking
flashing me back to *The Wizard of Oz*
Munchkins. I kid you not, ladies and gents—
because no way can you make stuff
this horse-opera-sultry up—I kid you not
that hot as I burn for words,
she *stifles* me plumb-dumbstruck
when she tells us that she is looking to trade,
straight-across, her (and I quote) "black stallion
for an Angus steer." She figures us
for a damsel-in-distress-rescuing threesome,
if ever she's laid eyes, *and leg,* upon such
knights-in-wrinkled-armor who could surely
service her agri-needs?

                    Charlie Seemann—
a name never before in the history of soft porn
so poetically impeccably apropos—Charlie
Seemann (I just have to say it twice) scribes
copious notes across a folded sheet
of Western Folklife Center letterhead—deep, wet
ink iridescent as hematite lipstick
agleam in the strip joint's black-light. Coy Gail
Steiger mimics the Tinman, rusted
stiff in his stupefied grin,
caught off guard again in a deluge
with lube can out of reach. And *I,*
(who shall remain anonymous)
lamenting the *anterior* motive behind this
delectable arabesque leg, this wanton gam,
in my Wranglered lap, *I,* oh-so-Wild-
Bill-Shakespeareanly-gallant
with gravitas, inquire, "But why,
dearest, demurest, pulchritudinous Lady, doth thou
desire to barter thy steed darketh
for said steer darketh?" To which she replieth,

"Dude. *Dude!* (gut-shooting me twice
with her synonym for greenhorn) To butcher
the son-of-a-bitch and eat it
bloody rare!" Her culinary edacity
throws open the flood gates
to both my libido and salivary glands. Savoring
her leg now fifty fleshy lecherous fold,
I blossom into roughstock chorus:
                                    "Weeee're

off to see the wizard, The Wonderful
Wizard of Oz…because-because,
because-because-*because*—
because-of-the-wonderful-things-
he-does…." Yup, I grant you—
a far cry from Curley Fletcher's
"The Strawberry Roan"? But
Curley Fletcher, I'll betcha, never fletched
a fetching leg *this* curvy! And how, *oh
how,* her very sinuous, very serpentine,
very, very, lissome, very lithe, limber limb—yes, this *very*
Munchkin-stockinged limb—burnished the chrome pole
mirroring the weird
faces of voyeurs, men *and* women,
alike, and even men named Gail, all
channeling from the abyss and chanting
in their vacuous heads the mystical
antithesis to the Maharishi's mantra

in chorale unison, "we *doan* need
no stu-pid brain, we *doan* need
no stu-pid brain."
                    Only in Elko—
Elko!—can any old rode-hard-
an'-put-up-withered, wizard Zarzyski
fathom his delusional self speed-dialing
*Angus Steer Emergency Leasing
& Delivery Service* from the Horseshoe Bar
at the drop of a triple-XXX beaver
hat! Only to be put on hold,
the entire barroom singing in unison
to the Arkansas Sinatra, Glenn Ohrlin,
crooning through the iPhone:
(Sung to "Home on the Range")
"Oh give me a town,
with chiv-al-*ree* so pro-found—
I'm not talking 'bout Eden or Oz—
where a gal needing beef
wears a g-string fig leaf,
while three paladins take up her cause…."
            ELKO!

*For Charlie and Gail, and especially for the
"cowboy storyteller" extraordinaire—heaven
bless her—who put the three of us to shame.*

CALICO FEVER BLUES

(Lyric—Recorded a Cappella, By Yours Truly)

He's got the calico fever blue-*oos*
From his Stetson to his horse's shoe-*oos*
No more "his," no more "hers"
No more singin' from his spurs
She left him with nothin' left to lose.

He's got the calico fever blue-*oos*
No more music in them ol' cows' moo-*oos*
She beat the heck out of his pride
Just like a steak that's chicken-fried
She left him with nothin' left to lose.

      What's a cowboy to do
      When she says "vamoose, we're through"
      When there's no more jangle-jingle-jangle?
      What's a buckaroo to do
      When she tells him "toodle-oo"
      Just when he thought he had her roped-n-wrangled.

He's got the calico fever blue-*oos*
His ya-hoos have turned to boo-hoo-hoo-*oos*
The Lonely Hearts Club way out here's
A thousand head of bawling steers
She left him with nothin' left to lose.

What's a cowboy to do
When she says "vamoose, we're through"
When there's no more jangle-jingle-jangle?
What's a buckaroo to do
When she tells him "toodle-oo"
Just when he thought he had her roped-n-wrangled.

He's got the calico fever blue-*oos*
She bucked him off with the Dear John new-*oos*
His poor ol' "Achy Breaky Heart"
Just made the Stupid Singles chart
She left him with nothin' left to lose.

He's got the calico fever blue-hoo-hoo-*oos*.

*For the Open Path Music recording studio crew, who
lied when they vowed, "We can make you sound
more like Johnny Mathis than Johnny Unitas!"*

POMES

I've played Vegas and I'm itching
to boldly say *no way* poetry ever will
outstrut, outbluff, outmuscle, outpoint,
outshoot, outpitch, outshimmy, outshine
cleavage—oiled and glitter-sprinkled,
hummocking erumpent and hogging the show
without having to utter into the mike
one bardic word. Yup, I'm talking *bonbons*,
bodacious *sets of tatas*, *bazongas*-to-the-button-
buster-max, flexed gibbous as the Governator's **biceps**—
pumped-up-push-up-cupped double-D bazooms
girded with *boost-T-yea* rebar. What jagged
brace of salient salacious stanzas can trump
these curvaceous plump pairs of eights
over ace-of-hearts kickers? What titillating
alliterative single line of lyrical literary verse
ever—since that first pomaceous babe, Eve,
bit, topless, into a crisp juicy Winesap
in Eden—*ever* eclipsed even one of these
rising full moons over Cancun?

No buts about it—*Vegas*, where, worse,
bunking above Mandalay Bay's Bay, I was
baited to peer down into the steamy
red, white, and blue cauldron of sex
soup. Not your brothy consommé, mind you,
but rather that Mafioso brothel-of-a-bowl,
cioppino. Cioppino Beach! Who here needs
a sestina? Who is left wanting for lack of
ballads, villanelles, those impotently stuck-in-
neutral, parked-legally-in-handicapped-zones **haikus**—
or, far more stiffless yet, that Viagra-deprived
limerick! Let alone the soporific, lopsided
Petrarchan sonnet. Thus, let us now ogle,
rather than talk, rhymed couplets, parallel
structure, alliteration-to-a-dangerous-duo-
décolletage-tee—silicone sibilance tossed in
for good measure. Hell, just give me an ode
on *two* Grecian urns, a Beauty *&* Truth tattoo,
its ampersand *and* echoing down the box
canyon of a cowboy poet's mind.

For Glenna Branagan and Denise Withnell—
the only two women friends I could
bribe into approving of this poem.

Cowpoke Cosmos Highs

LONG SAGEBRUSH DRIVES—
AN ADRENALINE-INDUCED, TESTOSTERONE-FUELED, BUCKIN'-HOSS-TWISTER, ROUGHSTOCKAHOLIC JABBERWOCKY-RAP

Six roughstock buck-offs in a land-barge Ford
Six riggin' bags cached in the trunk
Umpteen go-arounds, none of us scored
Our riggin's all leaked and we sunk—

With our ids and our egos all shrunk
We're bummered in a deep purple funk.

Hatful-o'-ones buys a full tank-o'-gas
Sack-o'-chew-n-a-two-pack-o'-beer
The good news is while five guys crash
One half-awake feller can steer—

Just punch him into Copenhagen gear
He'll forget about sheep and count deer.

      Six roughstock Trekkies on a Galaxy trip
      On our starry-eyed Enter*prise*
      We're doing Warp 8 on **LSD**—
      Takin' Long **S**agebrush **D**rives
      Talkin' Long **S**agebrush **D**rives.

Six roughstock winners in a one-horse town
Fort Knox in a twenty-buck room
Rosined-up hot testosterone
Leather-n-Libido perfume—

Tip your lid with its bird-of-prey plume
At The Casanova Cowboy Saloon.

Summers of love on the rodeo trail
Groovin'-to-LeDoux-rock-n-rowel
High-octane buckin' hoss cocktails
Jacked-up on the Wolfman's howl—

With the yellow-moon-eyed hoot owl
See a Peckinpah *Wild Bunch* prowl.

    Six roughstock rounders orbiting the West
    Like nectar bees circling hives
    On our sweet-tooth quest for **LSD**—
    Takin' Long Sagebrush Drives
    Talkin' Long Sagebrush Drives
    When and where, but no whys
    On our Cowpoke Cosmos highs
    Across tie-dyed sunset skies…

    Takin' *Loooonnngggg…*Sagebrush…*Dri-i-ives.*

For Roughstock Rapper, Ramblin' Jack Elliott

SUPER-GROOVING IN THE "VOODOO LOU"

> *"The rock's easy, but the roll is another thing."*
> Keith Richards

Even the wind we bucked
is blown away
by million-decibel Rolling
Stones (nope, not singing Bob Nolan's
"Tumbling Tumbleweeds")
reverberating from hatchback to hood
latch of our compact
car whizzing like a full-metal jacketed
hundred-grain projectile
between Ely and Elko. We are taking LSD—
Long Sagebrush Drives—
through a people-less
space that would bloody bummer-trip
Mick and Keith from their beauty
of a bluesy combination plate
pharmaceutical-booze high. Rocking
to lewd lyrics in the rolling
"Voodoo Lou," we name Her
for Her black magic knack to make it
to the next station, nothing
sloshing in Her tank
but a gasoline flashback. Call this
unbridled love
for the sexy sixties. Say we are

a secret missile being
tested by The Cowboy
Poetry Conspiracy
in Nevada, land of the clandestine—
land blasted to smithereens
by the megaton munchies-crazed psych-*oh-oh-*
delic mushroom-clouded minds
of no rhyme nor reason—land of high
desert home
where The Incredible
Burning Man roams, of blue lane
laser travel by two
jazzed-up fanatic
shoot-the-moon lunatics
wagering it all, with crap table odds,
against a static gas
gauge needle on **E**
as we unabashedly talk
vegetarian chuck and cowboy
music in a culture
shock of confused fission
or fusion gone awol
to the meter-less beat of Mick
Too-Slim Jagger crooning
"Sparks *will* fly
all the way from **E**-*LYE*"
while we, Geiger counters crackling
wild in the Voodoo Lou, do, too.

For Trish O'Malley

RODEO POET BARNSTORMER

"Ain't no money in poetry
That's what sets the poet free
And I've had all the freedom I can stand."
Guy Clark
"Cold Dog Soup"

Eighty-nine copies of your latest
alliterative *lariati* title—
sans remaining space for one more
iambic molecule of mold or mildew, one more
fly-poop-period-gone-wild black speck—
crammed into the Genuine Split Cowhide
suitcase you finagled
out of your widow neighbor in trade for
your soon-to-be-released spoken-word 8-track
at her "Moving-To-Rest-Home Living Estate Sale,"
you fly Loop-The-Loop Airlines
to your next big gig. In your head,
you rehearse in pig Latin—straining
to *maybe* make them funny—the same ten epic
poems you loosely remember
thinking up decades ago. Their Rip van Winkle
barbiturate-laced-with-melatonin potency
clotheslines you into REM sleep
so primal, you dream that you dream
that the aft luggage hatch, un-puckered
as the prolapsed sphincter of *Pterodactylus*,
dumps your poetic fusillade down
like lutefisk and lefse on the land
of "the other white meat." Outside Dubuque,
dewlapped men in bibs and hip boots,
after the runic deluge, peel pages

off the sides of silos. *Hog Gazette*
headlines read: **PLUTONION SPACECRAFT
BREAK-UP OVER DUBUQUE
SCATTERS DOGGEREL DEBRIS**. You wake up
to the flight attendant's "*buh*-bye, *bub*-eye,
bub-bye" refrain, spring for a two-hour
five-block cab ride, sign one free
glossy press photo after your show,
get hornswoggled into swapping
with slam cowboy poets from the Bronx
your leather-bound limited editions
for their mimeographed pamphlets, and swear—
digging into a 4 a.m. La Guardia garlic-
prosciutto-arugula-Asiago-giardiniera
vending machine omelet—
never, ever, to wangle
your waddie way back east again.

For Spike Barkin

THE PASSION OF THE TOAST

Now let us pray and let us pay
kudos to the new flimflammer champ
of the entrepreneurial universe, you
shrewd epicurean sous-chef to The Big Guy,
you. *You*, who oleo-margarined cheap white bread
sparingly enough not to tear it,
then experimented with Teflon over gas
flame dialed to high heaven—
for forty days and forty nights, give or take
a fortnight—until the grilled American
partially-charred cheese
sandwich harkened its illusion, cast
its spell upon the *"Holy Moses!"* chosen few
most bamboozleable souls.
                              Easy to believe
you sold such sacrosanct
folk art on eBay for twenty-eight-smooth-
root-of-all-evil Gs. Hallelujah,
pass the mazuma, and God bless
Brother Rorschach's reverse take on this
perfect Virgin Mary framed—
rather gothically, wouldn't you agree?—
in burnt dough. On the flip side,
I'd say it's safe to say, isn't it,
"perspective *is* the devil's workshop?
Vantage point rules the roost? Beauty
indeed is in the skewed view
of the behold*en*, etcetera, yadda-yadda-
yadda, etcetera?"
                              In other words,
for my priestly-sober, oxymoronic,
hoaxable simoleons,

this golden-brown bleached blonde
resembles more the virgin-*less*
Andy Warhol portrait of Marilyn Monroe
burgeoning from the bread. For *her*, by God,
I'd have bumped the bid up
to twenty-eight-double-ought-one,
got more bang, so to speak, for my buck,
cloned the toasted-cheese
miracle by the millions into a "He
Works-In-Mysterious-Ways"
line of microwavable airline
TV dinners: "You'll go Gaga over
our new Provolone Monte Cristo
Monroe, our *un*like-a-virgin Fish-stick Madonnas,
our finger-lickin' Brittany Chicken Spears—"
sinfully mortal last meals to be savored
piping hot as are you, spiraling down
in fictional flames while glued
to the latest designer news-
flash from the super-
duper network,
Foxy Babe.

For Mike Husband and Judy Heberling—Epicurean
friends who would never *risk charring*, especially,
a grilled American *"cheese" sandwich!*

My Cattywampus Noggin

"WHY *I* AM NOT GOING TO BUY A COMPUTER"

*A man was coaxed out of his home by police after he pulled
a gun and shot his personal computer.… "We don't know if it
wouldn't boot up or what," Sgt. Keith Moon said. The computer
had four bullet holes in the hard drive and one in the monitor.*

*Associated press
Issaquah, WA
(c. 1994)*

Because pitching woo to my 1952 baby
blue Smith-Corona Silent-Super—good ol' U.S. of A.
steel and iron, truer than a shoeing anvil—is like
getting mighty western on a saddle
blanket in the hayloft on a cool July afternoon,
rain clacketing cedar-shake rhythms
with a woman simply reliving all
the horseback gaits—a trick-riding,
bale-bucking, jitterbugging, windmill-climbing, cayuse-
chasing, sharpshooting, wild-and-woolly-bully
take-that-extra-grip-and-let-'er-rip
red-and-black-ribboned pony-tailed Annie
Oakley in pearl-button blouse
unsnapping with the sound of keys
striking any letters to the platen
and her Wrangler jeans unzipping,
so willingly unzipping, and unzipping
with each gentle fingertip stroke of her
curvaceously chromed carriage-return lever. *Yes. YES!*
I love the white tongues of 50-bond
rolling into her, love to set her touch selector on
HEAVY, to experiment with her page gauge—
all her features A-B-C-D-*EZ*,

like the difference between sensing
what's primordially done
the first time out of the cardboard box
and having to shout "TIME OUT!"
over and over to read and decipher
the "how to satisfy your cyclops cyborg mate"
umpteen-hundred-page omnibus volume
printed in teeny Japanese
because your plastic 10K-per-day Cover Girl model
will expect you to know her RAMs and ROMs
and secret hieroglyphic code to her
single kilobyte G-spot combination
until you become a demolitions expert with the D.T.'s
trying to defuse, "eeny-meeny-miney-mo" all of her
falsie microchips filled with all of her fits
of frigidity, the *Apple* of your eye
click-clicking her tsk-tsk-tsk
disapproval at you through pretentious teeth—
one wrong function-key tweak or lick, one
power surge or instamatic camera flash
from shutterbugging God, one wrong
fondling of her mouse, and it's kiss
her "hope-we-can-still-be-user-friendly"
floppy-disc memory
of all your precious, sweet words
Good-Bye!

For Wendell Berry—This Cowboy
Spin-off of His Essay by the Same Title

THE "HAVE LAPTOP, WILL TRAVEL" PALADIN-NEVER-USED-A-COMPUTER BOOGIE-WOOGIE BLUES

(Lyric—Recorded by Greg Keeler)

Got a laptop dallied to the apple of my saddle
I'm moving stock and talking with my broker in Seattle
I'm a yahooin' dot-commer
Don't tell the Unabomber
I'm a cyberspace roughrider
I'm a rammer and a rommer.

Got software in my bedroll and a mouse tucked in my pocket
Named my pony Billy Gates, though he used to be Blue Rocket
I'm a zoomed-in buckaroo
I punched-up "cock-a-doodle-doo"
On my *Cowboy Poe-em* program
Next to "chicken noodle stew."

Got Windows in my saddlebags, a slicker full of floppies
Rhyming circles 'round Zarzyski who still types on ol' jalopies
I'm filthy rich with kilobytes
And oh-my-god what thrilling nights
When we boot-up in the bunkhouse
To those naughty triple X'er sites.

Got my hat and chaps on eBay, my partners all have email
My 3-pronged 'lectric lariat's a long ways from a female
I'm techno-rancher-maximum
Don't ship my calves, I'm faxin' 'em
I used to have a cattle herd
But now I just have stacks of 'em.

Got a psychedelic screen saver that flies me high as Saturn
Sure beats those nights we'd toke too much, then watch the ol' test pattern
With virtual reality
Calves bring a dollar-ninety-three
While packing house executives
All stand in line for cheese that's free.

Got a hard drive in the hand-hold of my linked-up bareback riggin'
I'm online and I'm draggin' while my bronco is a-ziggin'
My spurs are double-clickin'
Can't download me, I'm stickin'
With desktop equine interface
The icon is a chicken.

Got my monitor all wall-papered with Bullets, Roys, and Triggers
Got a blinkin' built-in cursor, now it damn sure friggin' figures
                    (*slower / ritardando!*)
Cuz my bushwhacked West just went plumb black

No menu for to take me back

To my true-blue Smith-Corona
With Her steady clack-clack...clack...clack...*claaaack.*

RODEO POET HORSE-MANURE-FORKER

Not your run-of-the-mill manure,
no sirree—these are creative greenbacks
in the round, wads of quadruple sawbucks, hard
cold October simoleons, ingots
alchemized, frozen into gold
bullion bouncing off
fartknocker Fort Knox
terra firma. You fork and shovel
tractor bucketfuls. "Booty, plunder, loot,
doubloons," you hear the most
horseshit-delusional snake oil salesman
part of your swashbuckler self
barking, as you rake it in and pile it
high as hay you paid two months' wages for. Manure,
hay. Hay, manure. *Ars poetica*
agronomics. Because it takes manure
to make manure, which makes hay
while the sun shines. Kind of
like ashes to ashes, like what goes
around comes around—old road-apple
planet earth rotating
on its pitchfork tine axis, perfect
metaphor from your saloon hall gal
muse with her soothing
"ma-*nure*, ma-*nure*, ma-*nure*"

mantra she wants you to ruminate
the deep-hidden, shit-eating-grin
meaning of. Thusly inspired—
your arm thrown over the 16-hands-high
withers of this rhythmical word
rewarding a job well-rhymed—you nicker and *neigh*
each stinking-rich step of the *way*
home to the poetic bank.

For John and Robbin Dofflemyer

THE DAY MY DENTIST, GEORGE OLSEN, WAS CROWNED "HERO!" TO POETS ACROSS THE WHOLE COWPOKE COSMOS

Tilted topsy-turvy and periodontically probed
for hours—launched by a laudanum-
Novocain-nitrous oxide bronc called Cocktail
toward the planet Amalgam—I have just begun
my tipsy re-entry into atmospheric earth
when George, steering me into the staff lunchroom,
props me like a cryogenic med-school cadaver
up against the candy bar dispenser. Through paint-
shaker gallons of latex-red retinas, I greet
identical triplet hygienists, receptionists,
dental assistants, janitors, patients recruited
from adjacent offices, and vagrants and patrons
the overeager doctor carnival-barked
across the parking lot from the casino
next door. George, beaming his neon
keno-machine smile—so blinding,
he does not need examination lamps
over his tandem rows of dental chairs—
politely beckons, "Paul, would you be
so kind as to recite for us a cowboy poem?" I,
hemming and hawing, but seeing merely double
by now, reply, "Gee-whiz, George,
thank you for this Carnegie Hall-esque venue,
this captured—I mean *captive*—audience,
but every poetic corpuscle is still
clogged in my cattywampus noggin,
like wet sand in the upper bulb of an hourglass,

and, well, though I hate to say *no*...
I...I..." and then, ay-yi-yi-yi-yi, I remember
the wisdom teeth extractions, and gingivectomy,
and pulp testing of numbers 3 and 14
back-to-back with two root amputations
scheduled next week. "My pleasure!"
I effervesce, breaking into verse
making the packed roomful flash
their simonized, perfectly-aligned,
pearly-white grins. Not, however,
one bit, *or bite*, as lustrous
as the '52 Buick grille of chromed ivories
I gleam when feasting my eyes
upon the double double-ought zeros
at the bottom of my itemized bill—in bold
growling saber-toothed caps beside the entry,
Means of Payment: *P O E T R Y.*

For George, Faye, Dee, and the Gang

125

PRE-OP-POET BLUES

"*NOTHING* to eat or drink after midnight"
puts the Yosemite Sam "*WHOA!*" on my morning
tryst with the Muse who knows she comes
second only to my first cup of joe—the caffeine
fix my very Italian mother hooked me on
when she laced my baby bottle with "just *a little*
dribble," from her coffee cup
because of the adorable way it made me
chortle. My Muse agrees—
I *am* far more oral-to-the-robust-max
when caffeinated. Sixty years of a.m. java
turning the creative ignition
switch to my 8-banger ticker
and, *now*, nary a *click-click-click*? My shocked
corpuscles succumbing
to this torture, the Muse arrives to find
not Zippy Zarzyski, but Zombie Zarzyski,
drooling down the front of his Edgar Allen Poe
pajamas—a bottomless grave of blank page
glowering up at him. What sawtoothed lines
worth a waltzing grain of salt would ever
show their cadenced faces
to one so catatonic—would *ever* squawk,
raven-hopping-mad with inked claws
across the poet's opened Moleskine notebook
breathed upon with breath so insipid, so
devoid of *caffé stretto*? Alas, in light of my usual
"Jack and the *Coffee* Beanstalk on Steroids"
horticulture of colossal stanzas
stacked into the stratosphere, what

in the flaming Hades' gardens of deep space *is this*
bardic-toadstool ditty of a poem
I've germinated here with mere
fumes of my former torrid self? All
while the surgeon, likely steeped in his
Swimsuit Issue of *Barista Babe Magazine,*
hotshots his nerves with a third quadruple-
sugar-cubed triple espresso? Could it be he knows
how the caffeinated-to-the-agitated-max
scalpel hand damn well *better be*
in jittery sync with the caffeine-deprived
Mafioso-poet's pen-wielding trigger finger
hand he'll be operating on? Shaking
like a Jimmy Hoffa coffee-tree leaf?

For Dr. Chuck Jennings—Maestro of the Knife,
Virtuoso of the Suture

Swimmin' The Cow*boy* Fountain Of Youth

HOW THE LORD THROWED-IN WITH MOM
TO MAKE ME QUIT THE BRONCS

'Twas as my mother sayin' rosaries day and night
—beads coiled 'round each mitt—
that compelled the Lord to heed her prayers,
if He built this world in seven days
He could dang sure make me quit.

So first God hires on this angel,
a thief, a rustler, 'fore he come reborn,
to filch my war bag from the pickup cab—
"no gear, too broke to buy it new," God thought,
"*that'll* ear him down and leave him shorn."

Now I got no insurance on my life,
my health, my house, or half-ton Ford,
so when State Farm rushed that check
—full coverage for my losses—
you might say, it *surprised* the Lord!

Inside a week, I'm back a-scratchin'
with riggin', hooks, rosin, chaps, and glove,
while God, studyin' hard his notes
on Rodeo—"How to break an addict"—
concocts plan B there up above.

"I'll hang him up," He figures, "spook him good,
have Kesler's Three Bars stomp his lights,
pop his stubborn pumpkin off arena posts
'til he's floppin' like a neck-wrung chicken—
that'll squelch his fight!"

Now spurrin' bares is a bunch of fun
when you're gettin' holts and packin' extra luck,
but when you're hung, your riggin's slipped,
and you're downstairs, it's a lot like slap shot,
hockey—your noggin plays the puck.

That mare rag-dolled me 'round the arena,
left me caked with lather, blood, and dirt,
and yeah, I took some stitchin' up,
but even worse, my ridin' arm's much longer now—
it's a *bitch* to tailor me a shirt.

I'll hand it to the Lord on this one,
He come close to sourin' me for good,
but "close" don't count for nothin'
'cept in pitchin' hand grenades and horseshoes—
next day, I enters every rodeo I could.

When plans C thru V don't work no better
and the Almighty's runnin' shy of rope,
He savvies *W,* for *Woman,* "I'll make
that twister fall so hard in love and lust..."
she'd make me hang 'em up, He hoped!

Oh, she was the prettiest filly God give teeth
—next to her, Bo Derek scored a 2—
and I quit everything she asked,
from snoose, to hootch, to cussin' rank,
but no, not buckers, no matter how she'd coo.

So finally mom stopped prayin', and God's relieved,
cuz He run out of plans with Z,
ol' Three Bars, she's retired, my gal's run off,
and you know, I'll be go-to-hell
if everyone ain't up and quit, **but me**!

> *In Memory of my Dear Mom, Delia, who had hoped beyond all hope that
> her firstborn would become "either a priest or a doctor married to an
> Italian nurse"—never in her most nightmarish dreams, a rodeo poet.*

DEAR MOM

"Please don't tell my mother I'm a rodeo cowboy. She thinks I play piano at the whorehouse in Wallace, Idaho."

The night that devil danced on me
I know how you barely peeked
between fingers and beads. You heard
the hard blow-by-blow
announcer cawing from the crow's nest,
above the cowboy holler and dust,
how I was hung and being drug
by a bronc no one could stop. No,
Dad should *not* have brought his gun,
and I doubt your rosary
will salvage me from hell. You bet
I can remember
how you massaged my gums
with homemade hootch
to ease the teething,
how you never dreamed
that twenty-three years later
a palomino bronc name Moonshine
would leave me toothless in Missoula.

BENNY REYNOLDS' BAREBACK RIGGIN'

A bacon slab a-boiled black in oil every day
Ain't as soggy as the surcingle he folds whatever twisted way

He wants to, heck it always has sprung back
Like a flapping magic bird pulled from his riggin' sack,

Pre-rosined, and fit directly to the withers of a bare
As if slipping on his socks, there's never any scare

In his wrinkleless face—those are laugh lines!—
And no matter what he draws, he never frets or whines

Or paces, he just climbs aboard and shakes his face
And takes to raking like he's in a race

To stay one big lick ahead of old-man time
Who can't figure any reason, can't savvy any rhyme

To the way this rodeo-arena George Burns
Keeps on smoking 'em, how he never learns

That he's older than petrified dinosaur poop—
Did he "Cowboy?" or did he "Caveman?" with Alley Oop

Back when he and glaciers together first cracked out
In the Mesozoic era when stock was Flintstone stout

When you had to strap a muzzle on Tyrannosaurus Rex
Or you'd lose a leg or two, and talk about your wrecks!

Those pile-driving reptiles hit the ground with force
And mass a thousand times that of a feathered horse

Bounced a fan from front row to a nosebleed seat
You had to get your holts, you had to use your feet

Whether you was entered-up, or you was there to watch
Benny Reynolds setting this same riggin' in the scaly notch

Between the first and second spike-ed dorsal fin
Of some big ol' thorny lizard he spurred hard enough to win

Just like he does today, with lots of rapid gap,
Those dinos had some girth so you damn sure had to tap

Off on that first squalling hop, or good-bye screws
That snub your riggin' handhold to its body, and you'd lose

Your gripper, and get back-doored and likely whaled,
A shuttlecock badmintoned by a thrashing three-ton tail!

Which is why, I'll bet, three wraps of rusty baling wire
Is what's holding Benny's handhold on, I could inquire

But I hate to seem a greenhorn, wet behind the ears
Regardless of the umpteen hundred dozen years,

Or eons, that separate our riding gear and style
Of psyching-up—I'm a nervous wreck, Benny's one big smile!

And once I even seen him place a snoosey, juicy smooch
Upon the cheek of Kesler's pick-up man, not even hooch

Could loosen me enough for such flamboyant flare and flirt—
Besides, I mostly pick myself up, I mostly kiss the dirt.

But *why?* My riggin's up to date with each space-age part
Tailor-made, fit-to-form, state of the art

High-tech precision, the bareback Cadillac of rigs
Aerodynamically perfected like the Rooskies build their MiGs

Not prehistoric pterodactyls, the only thing that flew
Awkward as a tailless kite, back when Benny's rig was *new*!

It's time to shed some light upon this riddle I've got spun,
I'll rub the maker's stamp with spit and tilt it toward the sun

I swear it won't surprise me, I'm ready to believe
It's built at Adam's Saddlery from snake hide tanned by Eve.

For Benny and Tex Smith

RODEO IN HIS BONES

(Lyric Precursor to "Rodeo to the Bone"
Recorded by Wylie Gustafson)

He rocked-n-roweled for eons
With The Cowpoke Rolling Stones,
But Bronco Rock, once in his blood,
Now yodels in his bones.
Cattywampus posture
A knee that squeaks-n-squawks
A jug of Redeye Lubricant
Can't change the way he walks.

Compound and hairline fractures
From six Strawberry Roans
Rearranged his DNA
Kinked his chromosomes.
Kinfolk to The Missing Link
He's Stone-Age pedigree—
A woolly mammoth-whisperer
Sits in his family tree.

       He's a Rambo, he's a Rocky,
       He's a rodeo Stallone,
       A bronco-stompin' honky-tonkin'
       Indiana Jones—
       He's an X-ray motion picture,
       Rodeo is in his bones.

His nose, his cheeks, his lower jaw,
The few teeth he still owns—
All relocated by the bull
They call Ol' Facelift Jones.
His forehead's now a fivehead
Titanium and screws—
No other creature like him
Not on Star Trek or in zoos.

Hunched forward like he's Sasquatch,
He drags his knucklebones
Like climbing up Mount Rushmore
With a backpack full of stones.
He's a chiropractic snafu,
An orthopedic wreck
Of spinal column fusion
From his tailbone to his neck.

His hide looks zipped together,
He's been stapled-up and sewn—
Mary Shelley's Frankenstein
Meets The Twilight Zone.
A tie rod in each femur,
New ball joints in each hip—
His doctor and mechanic
Had to form a partnership.

He's a Rambo, he's a Rocky,
He's a rodeo Stallone,
A bronco-stompin' honky-tonkin'
Indiana Jones—
He's an X-ray motion picture,
Rodeo is in his bones.

A walkin' talkin' musical,
"Rodeo Right To the Bone."

For Wylie, and for Billy Stockton

THE ROUGHSTOCKAHOLIC'S "JUST-ONE-MORE-LAST-ONE" BLUES

What I would pledge for one more horse?
I'd drive a Rambler, scrap the Porsche.
I'd swear off beef and live on borscht.
And I'd improve my rhymes, of course—
I'd dee-vorce free-verse for that horse.

What I'd do for just one bucker?
I'd pull a knife on an oyster shucker.
Throw back the trout, and keep the sucker.
Sell the cows, start ranchin' cluckers—
I'd hang-glide Baghdad for that bucker.

What I would don for one last nod?
I'd don a tutu upon my cod.
Don kilts and moon you while I shod.
Across *this stage* in jodhpurs trod—
I'd don pink Carhartts for that nod.

What I'd try for one last fannin'?
I'd try my Nikes, never ran in.
I'd try my hand at farmin' salmon.
I'd try a *real* hat on Hal Cannon—
I'd try wine coolers for that fannin'.

What I would quit to spur one more?
I'd quit the pies I eat galore.
I'd mum's the word, my girlfriend snores.
Quit shootin' polecats through the floor—
Well, I *might* quit pies to spur one more.

What I would swap for just one bronc?
My Buckhorn Beer for Chenin Blanc.
Ol' Dunny's nicker for a honk.
"Swap gun for club," just call me *Gronnkk*—
I'd walk on knuckles for that bronc.

What I'd do once more to gas-it?
I'd breed my heeler to a basset.
A **Free Beer!** sign? I'd shrug and pass it.
Tell MasterCard to kiss my asset—
I'd liquidate once more to gas-it.

What I'd risk for one last lick?
I'd hand-feed pumas tofu sticks.
I'd call the sumo champ "a plick!"
My girlfriend's barrel horse, I'd quick—
I'd risk *pure* fury for that lick.

One nod, one bronc, one lick come true—
One more last ride, I *swear* I'm through.
No more whinny, no more moo.
I'll move down under—I'll *buck a roo!*
Did I say "one"? Let's make that "two."

For Hal Cannon and Meg Glaser—
to the early Elko years (when ditties
like this brought the house down).

A COWBOY REEL

"Ain't a hand been hatched since 1950,"
you'll hear some real cowboy pontificate and pine—
"just a bunch of wanna-bes,
Hopalong-come-latelies,"
compared to him, who's born, of course, in 1949.

The real cowboy's rare as hen's teeth,
as watermelons vine-ripened in Alaska—
extinct as Brontosaurus,
on the plains or in the forest,
but these purebloods, they'll just brashly up and ask ya,

"Ever seen a gen-u-wine, authentic, real cowboy?
Who rides a real rank real mustang to head and heel?
A true waddie, a ranahan,
a leather-poundin' cavvy-man?"
Well, maybe not, but I have seen a cowboy reel

From the deck of a pitchin' green-broke colt,
while spin-fishin' in the middle of Flat Crick.
It was back in '83,
who cares what century
when you watch a boiled-over pony jump and kick,

Because my partner set all his hooks
into a missile of a fish *and* his horse, who followed suit
with acrobatical gyration,
no room for arbitration—
this scene reincarnated 'neath Charlie Russell's butte,

Where my partner lives, and lives to eat
and hunt and fish and ride with all his heart.
I could hear his belly growlin'
through the rockin' and the rowelin'—
he was set on havin' charcoaled cutthroat a la carte.

Now it's true that Flat Crick ain't the Mighty Mo,
but she's roily and she's knee-deep on a leggy hoss
who's fightin' for a holt
with every bolt and jolt
over boulders, loose and round and slick with slimy moss.

But my partner keeps on reelin' with both hands,
while ridin' Rooster Cogburn-style in a fight—
the reins are in his teeth,
Moby Dick is underneath,
but he's holdin' rod-tip high and his drag is set just right.

By now, that colt's a whirlybirdin' blur,
with monofilament a-racin' underneath his tail—
a helicopter Pegasus,
more Big Spins than six Las Vegases!
We later named this dance "The Bronco Bail,"

Which, on a fishin' reel, is the part that guides the line,
and my partner's bail is smokin' somethin' mean—
sons-a-bitchin' friction
(Please excuse my diction)
from drag to croup the shittin' line's a streak of neon green.

So this is what it means to *horse* a fish,
'stead of playin' him slow and easy to the bank.
When four hooves hit terra firma,
like the hurricane named Irma,
that fish slapped smack against that horse's flank,

Which sent the trio trollin' through thin air,
in Montana, where daredevils make their home.
In the eye of this upheaval,
more Evel than Knievel,
I know I saw a sure-enough *reel* cowboy roam.

Does my bad spellin' discombobulate the question?
"To reel, or *not* to reel?" still rings a bell.
To all you bellyachers,
be you *reel* or be you fakers,
'til you've fished while pitchin', there just ain't no way to tell.

For Curt Stewart—Hell, he's still out
there "trollin' through thin air."

142

AIN'T NO LIFE AFTER RODEO:
THE POLISH-HOBO-RODEO-POET'S COMMENCEMENT
ADDRESS—TO THE CHAGRIN OF EVERY GRADUATE'S
MOTHER—AT THE COLLEGE OF BUCKAROO KNOWLEDGE

There ain't no life after rodeo
Sulled-up old cowboys will tell you so

So when you feel your spur-lick weaken
And your bareback riggin' goes to leakin'

Bury your gripper elbow-deep
To hell with lookin' before you leap!

Fight for those holts, sight down that mane
Spit in the face of age and pain

Give that hammerhead a hardware bath
Dazzle the judges with 90's math

Spur the rivets off your Wranglers
A cappella rowels don't need *danglers*

Rake like a maniac, tick for tick
Tip your Resistol, flick the crowd's BIC

Fast-feet-fast-feet, gas-it-n-mash
Toes turned out with each jab-n-slash

Insanity, love, plus aggression
Call it passion, call it obsession

Adrenalined fury, 200 proof
Like guzzlin' moonshine up on the roof

Runnin' on Bute, LeDoux songs and caffeine
You rollickin', rosined-up spurrin' machine

Too lazy to work, too scared to steal
Slavin' for wages bushwhacks your zeal

So charge that front-end for those 8
You ain't no rodeo reprobate!

Grit each stroke out with every tooth
You're swimmin' the cow*boy* fountain of youth

Love that sunfish and love that high-dive
Believe you will ride 'til you're 95.

In Memory of Chris LeDoux, and for Roughies
Everywhere—The Quick and the Dead

WASHED-UP ZARZYSKI RIDES OL' '65 MAYTAG TO A SUDSY STANDSTILL

Its spin cycle, exactly like my psyche,
maniacally out of centrifugal whack,
thus triggering this seismological
tectonic breakfast plate shift
at the epicenter of our house, the kitchen,
all-a-tremor in a seven-point-*oh-oh*
Richter scale quake, I sprint
down the hall—from my jiggling
eggs just *this* instant flipped
picture-book-perfect
over-easy in the cast iron skillet—
to hop aboard, for ballast,
the big white bus with all wheels
out of balance, the square-prowed scow
pounding upstream on the Colorado,
the Cape Canaveral space capsule
manned by chimpanzee
me during blast-off!
           A far, *far*
cry from Slim Pickens as Major Kong
screaming "**Yaw-*Hoo*! Yaw-*Hoo*!**"
while fanning with his Stetson
the nuke he forked out of the bomb bay doors
in *Dr. Strangelove*, I, in Dr. Strange*life*,
sit here simply sulking
while my once-jovial Sunday morning yolks
morph into calluses on the balls
of Sisyphus's feet.
             Like slipping
six bits into a Route 66 motel
Magic Fingers bunk gone berserk, I'm on high

vibrate for three gyrating minutes of rinse-
spin, a sure-enough cure for whatever ails you—
swollen prostate, bruised coccyx, prolapsed piles,
an acute case of the fat-ass, ED, VD,
Double Ds, LSD, PhD, LAPD, Medicare Plan D, all
while my agitated viscera mimics
what pink latex feels like
in the shaker at ACE!
                Singing, with vibrato,
my dirges to the gods of ignominious fate,
how, I ask you, does a Roughstock Pavarotti
mourning the loss of his former, far
more ebullient life than this
pissant existence of domesticity
not still picture his swashbuckler self
cinching his bareback riggin' to the withers
of Whiplash! Snake Eyes! Sky Rocket! Applejack!
Sally Rand! Creamo!
                Sliding off the slick white
top-loading lid of this flat-backed, hairless,
cyclopsed, multi-tailed freak of equine nature,
I *almost* catch myself *almost*
wishing for the very first time *ever*
I'd have *almost* gone instead to church?
                        Whoa

now, dude…**Mamma Mia!
It's a Miracle!** My sciatica
feels indubitably cured! *To boot*, I'll bet you
that our epicurean, horse-poop-eating Aussie,
Wolfgang Zeke, goes plumb-*doggy*-gaga
over these road-apple eggs? Not
to mention how today's six go-
'rounds of heavy bedding

will work wonders toward honing
my spur stroke—my "Authentic
Mr. Ed The-Talking-Horse Slippers" nickering
"Wil-*l-l-l*bur-*r-r-r*! Wil-*l-l-l*bur-*r-r-r*!"
every time their shaggy-napped heels
rowel their way up
ol' Maytag's enameled hide.
                              My good-luck
chartreuse Fruit of the Loom boxer-briefs
willing, and the Tide suds don't rise,
be sure to catch a blurred glimpse of me
as the All-Around (*and* around, *and* around)
Cowboy in the Sunday morn, soft *corn* porn,
hit video series—*Old Rodeo Geezer*
Bronc-Peelers Gone Wild-Assed Wild!—coming
soon to a Geriatric Appliance store near you.

For Walter and Shadd Piehl—
Father-Son Washed-up Roughies, a Pair

My Hopalong Godiva

NOT HAVING MADE IT AS A WRITER, ON HIS 55TH BIRTHDAY THE *POÉTE MAUDIT* TURNS HIMSELF IN TO LITERARY JOHNNY LAW AND, WHILE INCURRING THE THIRD DEGREE, FINALLY FESSES UP

Trust me, Lieutenant Hugo—I truly do not *know*
where my strumpet Muse goes now when She plays nooky
hooky, swooning under the radar on a Tuesday
afternoon, rather than her usual
Friday or Saturday night soirees, trysts,
liaisons that I *do* know She entertained
in our wooing years. Oh, you bet, did I *ever* fret,
stew, seethe, back when I did too much
pure uncut black-tar testosterone. *You* know?
From that number one most-wanted predator ever,
Mister Y chromosome, hanging around
playgrounds of adolescent male brain cells
and pushing the body's orgasmic chem lab
cocktails of ecstasy and crank? Power trip
quests-for-Big-Apple-success
wedding hubris with doubt
strutting down the pubescent aisle
hand-in-literati-hand? I did it, okay? I kept my Muse
tethered on a bungee-jumping leash
to the granite bed in the top turret
of my macho stronghold. Being male, being
whacked-out on stupid youth, are lame, I admit,
excuses. They don't hold sway in either
The People's Court *or* The Poets' Court. Thus, all
I ask now is to serve my sentence,
to pay my debt to the literary cognoscente,
in peace. Maybe She'll even forgive me.
Weirder things have happened, see? Maybe

She'll pay me a visit on my next birthday,
surprise me with a file, a hacksaw,
a jackhammer and jet-black getaway
Chevy muscle car—one strong line of poetry—
baked into the dynamite
filling of a deep-dish humble pie.

For Mark Gibbons—Fellow Poéte Maudit

THE MS. OF THE MEGA-MUNITIONS

She's got a shotgun under the loveseat
A Colt .45 in each drawer
A derringer tucked in her garter belt
Her boudoir is warrior décor.
Her mattress is literally ticking
Her bedposts are Tomahawk rockets
There's an Uzi beneath every pillow
She's got walk-in ammo closets.

Torpedoes are stacked in the bathtub
There's a blowgun that's made from a bone
A crossbow is cocked near the toilet
And her flamethrower looks like a phone.
She's got hot nitroglycerine faucets
Bandoliers festooning each room
There's a land mine under the WELCOME mat
Ring the bell, badda-bing badda-***boom***!

> She's the Ms. of the Mega-munitions
> She's sweet vigilante law
> She's a Bonnie Parker arsenal
> In *femme fatale* Shangri-la.
> The heiress to the hair-trigger
> Bouncing Betty of Vietnam
> She's feminine Armageddon
> She's a bombshell with the Bomb.

Her vestibule's filled with bazookas
There are mortars galore on her porch
A nuke submarine in her basement
Her powder room light is a torch.
There are ack-ack guns in her attic
A Sherman tank parked in her garage
Her pantry could pass for a battleship
Bon appétit and *bon voyage*.

The C-4 is stored in her parlor
Big Bertha is perched in her den
The smart bombs she keeps in her mezzanine
In the mudroom, dumdums for men.
With her atrium Minuteman silo
And her rooftop, a Cobra jet pad
With her B-52-cockpit greenhouse
She's the *last* gal you want to make mad!

She's the Ms. of the Mega-munitions
She's sweet vigilante law
She's a Bonnie Parker arsenal
In *femme fatale* Shangri-la.
The heiress to the hair-trigger
Bouncing Betty of Vietnam
She's feminine Armageddon
She's a bombshell with the Bomb.

She's a Bonnie Parker arsenal
In *femme fatale* Shangri-la.

SHE-DEVIL MUSE

> *"Why did God create men? Because*
> *vibrators can't mow the lawn."*
> Madonna

She pinned her tail on my donkey heart
She-played spin-the-*bot*-tle with my liver
She bushwhacked me at the "celibate social"
She loaded harpoons into Cupid's quiver—
She loaded harpoons into Cupid's quiver.

She sold my soul to the lowest bidder
She forged my name on Beelzebub's line
She slipped my minister a Mickey Finn
She Viagra'd my communion wine—
She slipped my minister a Mickey Finn
She Viagra'd my communion wine.

    Myyyyy...Beelzebabe in her halter tops
    My *un*-Lady Gaga in her meat dress chops
    My double-shot of Dante's Inferno Schnapps—
    She's a sh*eee*-devil, she's a sh*eee*-devil,
    But *oh sweet jeezuzz* she's **Hot! Hot! Hot!**

She *boobie*-trapped my guardian angel
She taught my cockatoo to curse-n-cuss
She un-torpedoed my speedo'd libido
She raised the Bismarck of my lust—
She raised the Bismarck of my lust.

She blew kazoo to my gospel music
She snored pornographically all night long
She played my rosewood Martin guitar
In her barbed wire bra and chain mail thong—
She played my rosewood Martin guitar
In her barbed wire bra and chain mail thong.

Myyyyy...Beelzebabe in her pink flip-flops
My Hopalong Godiva, clip-clop-clip-clop
My trollop with her habanero lollipops—
She's a sh*eee*-devil, she's a sh*eee*-devil,
But *oh sweet jeezuzz*, she's **Hot! Hot! Hot!**

She loco-weeded my mistletoe
She LSD'd my candy cane
She laid buck naked beneath my tree
With her gifts wrapped-up in Cellophane—
With her gifts wrapped-up in Cellophane.

She ukulele'd my Yo-Yo Ma
She Mother-Goosed my Aristotle
She glued into my Swimsuit Issue
My ex-wife's face on ev-er-y model—
She glued into my Swimsuit Issue
My ex-wife's face on ev-er-y model.

Myyyyy...double-shot of Dante's Inferno Schnapps
My trollop with her habanero lollipops
My choc'late bonbons with wasabi on top—
She's a sh*eee*-devil, she's a sh*eee*-devil,
But *oh sweet jeezuzz*, she's **Hot! Hot! Hot!**
She's a sh*eee*-devil, she's a sh*eee*-devil,
But *ohhhhhhh   sweet jeezuzz*   she's **Hot! Hot! Hot!**

*For Sande DeSalles—who begs me to write
more about men's relationships with women?*

WHY I AIN'T BUYING INTO
THE WORD "INSPIRATION"

As heavy-handed as gravity, the magnetic She-
force of poems pulls, bullies, baits,
solicits me to tag along,
to join Her for raw oysters and coitus,
for some bambalacha and a bump, to blast
some blond, do a doobie of sweet Lucy,
to get candy-flipping ripped, amped,
ring dang doo'd on succubus roofies,
on an Alice B. Toklas panful and a poke, *or*
for just a bit of chitchat over coffee—
posthaste, pronto, *now.* Far too often
I, refusing Her munificence, say, "Thanks
but no thanks, Ma'am?" I maybe doodle
a line or two, a shoot-from-the-hip
scribble for rainy days. But the Muse does not
do rain checks or futures, run bar tabs,
dole out go-cups, doggie bags or cash
advances. Her clip-n-save coupons all sport
the same ***right-this-frickin'-minute***
bold black expiration notice. Thin-skinned,
irascible, vindictive, She takes umbrage
even to the politest "no." She slaps me
out of hackneyed dreams at 3 a.m.,
hoists me from my counterfeit bliss
like Sister Mary Ivan, *un-*cloistered,
pried me from seat to tiptoes

with a Vice-Grip pinch to one ear. The Muse
knees me joyously in the groin, doubles
me over, embeds her instep into my forehead,
my wet lips pressed against Her
freshly pedicured nails
painted a shimmering, chatoyant,
cathouse candy-apple red. She makes me
whimper "give—okay I give!" She makes
my lips, ears, eyes, nostrils, fingertips
bleed for more—more euphoria, *more*—
as my first surge of words,
within ruled lines, penetrates, punctuates,
consummates this lust for She who is the one
and only runic seductress
intoxicating enough to trick
the light into the dark
exotic—the poem into the page.

For Poet Ciara Shuttleworth—may your relationship
with your Muse be every bit as "inspirational!"

BURN-BARREL PUBLISHING:
TO BURN OR *NOT* TO BURN? *THAT* IS THE QUESTION!

Just how much big-batch warm corn liquor
spilling into my tin-can cup
straight out of the still's copper coils
must I guzzle, *must* I gulp,
before I feast my seismic eyes upon
fancy decanter planet earth
tipping one nano-fraction on its axis
to fill my passion's empty cognac snifter
with Courvoisier? *How much*, as I'm about to strike a book
match to my expired manuscript (*this* poem
on page thirteen) drenched in gasoline,
kerosene, *Hustler* magazine, something
obscenely flammable, although poetry *is*
spontaneously—*don't* this world *know* it!—
combustible enough all on its own?
                              Just how much
aguamiel mezcal, how many pickled *gusanos*
will I kiss in, choke down, swallow whole
before I hallucinate
the sonic boom applause of all
winged insects within earshot
of my swan song? *How much*, as they exalt
in unison this literary fission, this fusion, this
fifty-five-gallon drum implosion of poems
rumbling to a standing ovation of one—**me**
catapulted from my folding lawn chair
alongside the red, white, and blue
beer cooler beneath the striped beach umbrella

under the moon and stars above the mushroom
cloud of strophic smoke and iambic ash?
                                        Just how many
screw-top Beaujolais-n-Smirnoff-Vodka snow cones
do I mainline with a siphon hose
straight into my Antarctic bardic marrow
before I ice my soaked-self sober
enough to learn? *How many*, only to learn,
yet again, how a seed-pit bullet
spit off my brisket by a dominatrix
muse ridiculing our break-up,
sparking the lock off my chained heart,
incites the defiant-word
riot of infinity's literal tinder
igniting me back into my wild-
assed dance, my line-by-jagged-on-the-right-line
lusting for firestorms of musical light?

For Allen Morris Jones

Chianti *Salutes*!

THE TUMBLEWEED MUNCHIES

After my nemesis, the stiff wind, howls,
under cover of darkness, "*Charge!*"
to her spiny urchin army of The Big Dry,
I find the scabrous bastards at first light
Velcroed by the battalion bunches
to every fenceline, shelterbelt, fissure, niche
of my choreful, not cheerful, life. "They might
have me surrounded, alrighty," I think,
wringing my hands, laughing my demonic laugh,
"but I have *them* cornered." I have
their roly-poly bouncy little backsides flattened
up against the wall. With my American Gothic
pitchfork held in bayonet stance, I thrust and tear
them away from their comrades,
stuff the spring-loaded cannon-fodder
sonsabitches into the 55-gallon burn barrel
coughing, choking, belching its thick brown
locomotive smoke until, *Poof*—"Fee-*Fry*-
Foe (especially Foe)-Fum"—it whooshes, then rumbles
with incendiary delight. Romping
around the crematorium, I begin to love
the last scratchings of their tumbleweed toenails
down the inside walls of the drum. I savor,
more and more, each intoxicatingly hot
peekaboo into their scanty ashen remains
glowering back up at me from the pulsing red
tuba's fumarole wherein this basso profundo
musical disintegration takes place. I can't wait
to ramrod the next forkful into the black
maw "making my day" every couple minutes,
cannabis-esque aromas hovering in the dusk,

as if Beelzebub, his far-out groovy self,
had rolled the mother of all doobies
in Tumbleweed Hell, where I find myself,
suddenly in a dead calm, smelling of hemp,
singed bald across both brows
and stricken with the inexplicable
severe craving for watercress tempura, fondued
baby squid, extra-extra-crisp, each bite
sizzling before my eyes upon the tines.

For Ed McClanahan and Gordon Stevens,
their "far-out groovy selves."

THE HEAVYWEIGHT CHAMPION PIE-EATIN' COWBOY OF THE WEST

I just ate *50* pies!—started off with coconut
macaroon, wedged my way through bar angel
chocolate, Marlborough, black walnut and sour cream
raisin to confetti-crusted crab apple—
still got room for dessert
and they can stick their *J-E-L-L-O*
where the cowpie don't shine, cause Sugar Plum
I don't eat nothing made from horses' hooves!

So make it something *pie*! Something light
and fancy, like huckleberry fluffy chiffon, go
extra heavy on the hucks and fluff, beaten
egg whites folded in just so. Or let's shoot
for something in plaid—red and tan lattice-
topped raspberry, honeyed crust
flakey and blistered to a luster, wild
fruit oozing with a scoop of hard vanilla!

Or maybe I'll strap on a feedbag of something
a smidgen more timid—quivering
custard with its nutmeg-freckled fill
nervous in the shell. Come to think of it now,
blue-ribbon mincemeat sounds a lot
more my cut—neck of venison, beef suet,
apples, raisins, citrus peel, currants,
all laced, Grammy-fashion, in blackstrap molasses!

No. Truth is, I'm craving shoofly or spiced rhubarb
or sure hard to match peachy praline,
cinnamon Winesap apple à la mode, walnut
crumb or chocolate-frosted pecan! *Or,*
whitecapped high above its fluted deep-dish crust,
a lemon angel meringue—*not* to mention
mandarin apricot, black bottom, banana cream,
burgundy berry or Bavarian nectarine ambrosia!

And how could you out-gun the Turkeyday
old reliables—sweet potato, its cousin
pumpkin, its sidekicks Dutch apple and cranberry
ice cream nut. *Ahhh*, harvest moon, that autumn
gourmet cheese supreme, or Jack Frost squash, or...
"my favorite," you ask? That's a tough one.
Just surprise me with something *new*, Sweetie
Pie! Like tangerine boomerang gooseberry!

For Larry Levinger, Curt Stewart, Joel Bernstein,
David Burnett, Jimmy Gammon, Bugs & Babe

STARBUCKS: PIE'S TANTO, PIE'S PANCHO, PIE'S SANCHO PANZA SIDEKICK *(a Jingle)*

When us cowboys see a shooting star,
"The Lone Ranger's missed again," we'll say—
"his aim is off by light years,
his silver bullet's gone astray."

He's drinking too much Arbuckles.
That ol' java makes him shake.
He ought to brew some Starbucks,
for heaven's western sake.

'Cause when a star *bucks* 'cross the sky,
we'll tell you that it means,
"Old cowboys savvied cattle brands,
but today *we know* our beans!"

BIZARZYSKI—MAD BARD AND CARPENTER SAVANT OF MANCHESTER, MONTANA— FEEDS THE FINICKY BIRDS

Unlikely that my poems will ever land
in some *Norton Anthology of Ornithology,* let alone
The Guinness Bird Book of World Bon Appétit Records,
I want all you Audubon *paesanos* to hear right now
who's the first mad poet to ring-shank-spike
a fat, foot-long, freezer-burned mule deer salami
to the icy top of a railroad tie corner post
where I distract rambunctious flocks
of ravenous magpies squawking happily all winter
away from the purple finch/English sparrow
birdseed feeders. Maybe I'm first
also to have learned that even a scavenger clings
to certain proprieties and will
exercise its right to decline a handout. Once,
I placed a frozen block of tofu
atop the very same post. No way. Not one minuscule
peck. Like offering *menudo*, pâté, haggis
to a vegan. Poor tofu—it didn't even get
a second look, a quizzical magpie glance
of comical disgust or surprise. I did not know
these birds could smell, let alone whiff
tofu at 30 below. I've watched
them gobble-up a bloated road-killed polecat
for brunch under a blacktop-softening sun. And so
it sat there, through five chinooks, through spring
and summer, until the post, I suppose, osmosised it,
almost, along with that dangerous duo

of Mafioso hit men, Sal Monella and his sidekick, Bocci,
who must've thunk they'd bag a bird or two. But nothing
bit the dust, just like nothing bit the tofu. Thus,
I must confess—because I'm Catholic
and therefore unfulfilled unless I'm bearing guilt—
that I prayed very hard for scavenger forgiveness
as they laid their beady eyes upon my latest
feast and spiel: "My name is Paul. I'll be
your server this winter. For your delight,
our hammered chef tonight has spiked,
in lieu of our usual alder-planked smoked salmon
on the menu, frozen chunk of venison
sopressa over creosoted post. It's free!
I'll be right back to take your order."

For Skip Avansino and Joe Sciorra
(Grazie! Grazie Tanto!)

SADLY—OH-SO-SADLY—I HAVE TO EXPLAIN *THE SOPRANOS* TO SOMEONE WHO JUST DOES NOT *CAPICE*

…you got it yet, *goomba*? I'm *Eye*-talian.
And what we *Eye*-talians do, see,
besides communion with the one and only
true God, who also just so happens to be
Eye-talian—"Vengeance is mine
sayeth the lord?" Therefore we *did*
invent the vendetta? —what we do,
we *Eye*-talians, is turn *sad*
into *mad*. That's our solemn calling, that's just
the way it is, see—*sad* into *mad*, but *then*,
mad into *glad*. And *glad* is when we eat!

Which is all to say, we work goddamn hard
at being sad. It's simple logic—badda-bing,
badda-boom. No *sad*, no *mad*. No *mad*,
no *glad*. No *glad*, no *mangia!* And we
all live to *mangia!* Am I right or am I right?
Good! You finally got it! It looks like
maybe I won't have to kill you after all
'ey? I'm so glad—pass the polenta!—I'm *so*
goddamn glad, *paesan*. Now let's eat,
and pray before we do, for something sad
to make us mad, again, by supper.

In Memory of James Gandolfini

169

ANTIPASTO!

The tongue loves *ANTIPASTO!* The linguini way
each button-mushroom syllable—gold
nubbin plucked from hardwood stump—lingers
toward the uvula, palate to lips
to palate. Say, "floret." Slowly
say, "ivory cauliflower floret. Min-i-a-ture
sweet pickle. Red bell pepper. Chickpea."
Say, "celery heart, albacore fillet,
pearl onion." And say, "ebony olive"—
that favorite we fought over
as kids. Only the Grade **A**
make Mom's cut to this concertino
of sauce—tomato, virgin olive oil, herbs—
put-up in pints, the red-orange
pantry rows. Shout, "*ANTIPASTO!*
Pass the *ANTIPASTO!*" Thrill the inner ear
to this belfry of syllables, church-bell
meals festive enough for triple table leaves,
for old-country crystal
chiming Chianti *salutes* "to family,
to Mom—good health!—for *ANTIPASTO!*"

For My Brothers, Mark and Gary

POTATOES

Unless they've been clandestinely launched whole
into orbit as a satellite welcome wagon
gunnysack toward alien good will,
unless I've been mispronouncing "sputnik"
all these years, the quartet of big reds
freshly forked from Dad's garden—
stowaways in my carry-on luggage
above our heads—might be the highest
flying spuds since Kitty Hawk. I do not believe
in happenstance, so when the strapping
young man in the window seat
insists on *Close Encounters of the Third Kind*
(note allusion here to mashed potato scene)
after I've already warned him "I'm a poet
running on no sleep"—a threat
that deters him not one tater tot iota—
"*touché!*" I think, as I buckle myself
in for the, unbeknownst to me at the time, starchy ride
and fire politely right back at the guy, "So
what is it *you* do?" As deadpanned
as the metal-detector deputy in bouffant
when I cautioned her not to nuke back into humus
the tubers I'm sending through her microwave,
he proclaims, with a bit of sinister
un-whispered boast to his tone, "*I
am a potato breeder.*" It's a good thing
I'm graced with greater control than you folks
listening to this true tale. I, at least, am able
to draw—with a dull molar, no less—
a Red Cross pint from my inside cheek,
to restrain my spasmodic bladder, to counter,

without a single twitch
of upper lip or brow, without one Adam's apple
bobble, "*Ahhh*, so you breed (long pause)
potatoes." Luckily, my celibate darlings, huddled
like the epitome of virgin innocence
in their brown paper sack, are out of earshot,
I think, until I hear, from above, a jumping bean raucous
guffaw over Fargo, en route to Great Falls,
Montana—thank God not that Sodom
and Gomorrah of spud-lust states,
Idaho. So this is how I learned every *in* and *out*
of the chipping business, and yes,
the skins, like livers, do absorb
pesticide and fertilizer residues, but not enough
to compel one to forfeit the roughage benefit,
unless the subcutaneous epidermal layer has turned
green and, therefore, toxic. Incidentally,
the scientific name, should you find yourselves
in future discussion with horticultural savants
is *Solanum tuberosum.* I drink six vodkas
on the rocks over Bismarck. "You got your Yukon
Golds, your Fingerlings and Yellow Finns, your Chieftains,
your Chippewas, Kennebecs, Burbank Russets, Early
Gems, your Colorado Longs and Pontiac Reds,"
you name it—this young fella has come eyebud-
to-PhD-eyebud with every creed, color, race,
model, make, nationality and post-mortem
transmogrification. Me? I'm French-and curly-
fried by the time we touch down
at midnight in Montana and I say "*buh*-bye,

my little sweet potato pie," to the stewardess
who refuses to return my perfectly rhymed *toodle-oo*
adieu—I'm scalloped, twice-baked, *platskied*, jo jo'd,
au gratined, shoestringed, mashed, colcannoned, vichyssoised,
hashbrowned and having green potato skin
hallucinogen flashbacks and, worse,
forecasts, as suddenly every Samsonite suitcase,
every garment bag, every nylon backpack
and canvas duffel *transmutates*, right before
my protuberant eyes, into bulbous burlap sacks
on the baggage carousel, where I stand—
"the world's number one vegetable,"
between Rod Serling and Stephen King—confused
and drooling, mesmerized by the big blue-
lettered logo stenciled to the front of every gunny:
   Zarzyski's Purple Mazurkas
    We Put the P-O-E-T in
    P O T A T O E S

     For Dr. Christian Thill—Thanks for the wild
    spud*nik ride, for this turbo-**tuber**-charged poem!*

No-Laughing-Gas-In-Hell Mad

TELEMARKETER MALEDICTION

Even your own mother would opt for obscene
collect phone calls from her parish priest
over hearing from you. "How *am* I
this evening?" you ask. I am Lucifer-
frothing-rabid-in-the-middle-of-a-root-canal-
with-no-laughing-gas-in-Hell mad. And you, doc,
are the puddle of fresh puke
my new Gucci boot splats into
on its first unlucky step out of the Monte Carlo
right in front of my very favorite
steakhouse—you concocted-from-bean-curd
meat substitute, you! You bone meal-stuffed-
hotdog factory reject, you! You
single-wide-trailer-hide-a-bed-pain
in the lumbar of our society. You are lower than
six a.m. Sunday leaf blowers,
than roadside disposable diaper
bundles. Lower than funeral procession
road rage. More useless even
than Day of the Dead organ donors,
San Quentin prison lost and found,
than particleboard hot tubs,
a street pimp's receipts at an IRS audit. You
commuter flight sumo seatmate
with halitosis and the hiccups. You hot-quit
intermission in the middle of a cliffhanger
love scene. You collapsed plastic-bladdered
box of Beaujolais. You Aqua Velva
aftershave hangover. You disintegrating
winning lotto ticket spitball

in the washing machine tub bottom, you,
you…you…YOU are more infuriating than
a black gnat hatch at a nudist weenie roast
but, yes, I'll *gladly* give you my MasterCard
number and PIN, buy whatever
you're calling at beer-thirty to hawk, if only
you will lend me your ear
long enough for me to loathe your foaming-
putrid-from-the-test-tube-lips,
slime-mold-science-gone-awry
bungled fungal beginnings
with *my* "once in a lifetime
special offer only *to you*"—***this poem***!

For Gordon Stevens, Tim Volpicella,
Scott Sorkin, and Lee Ray

ZARZYSKI CURSES THE BURNING OF HIS BRO, ZOZOBRA, "OLD MAN GLOOM"

With his red-hot grimace of teeth
glowing like a blast furnace grate,
with lunacy blazing in his pizza-pan pupils,
and his nose the size of an *horno*,
this forty-foot marionette could be my twin,
my dismal spitting image, my kindled
kindred spirit. Burning in effigy
for the sixty-first time, he kicks off
Fiesta de Santa Fe—the year's woes
up in smoke, as Zozobra,
flailing his triple-hinged arms, groans
into flames. We're talking hot-foot
gone hubs-of-hell ballistic, the tipsy crowd cheering
this inferno, this animated Roman candle, and the Fire
Dancer, who torched my somber compadre,
leaping like a maniac Tinkerbell
dressed in red leotard
beneath a hot shower of debris.
                              Is this a Salem
stake fry crossed with Mount Vesuvius
crossed with that Robert Service verse
"The Cremation of Sam McGee"
mixed with the Hindenburg revisited? Is this
the gloriously torrid dream
of that Texan daredevil, Red Adair,
or what? And what in pyromaniacal Hades
is wrong with a modicum of melancholy
anyway?
            Old Zozo—my morose amigo,
my bluesy fellow double-Z, fellow last-in-liner
for life's ration of jubilation,

my hibachied hombre in black
bow tie and billowing white cassock—
although my gloom does not yet hold
one lugubrious *luminaria* to yours,
on that fateful day my Polish-*Eye*-talian bones
spontaneously ignite, I'll join you
in this toast:
                    "Here's to combustible us,
to our home in the doldrums. May our ashes,
blowing together as one glum
cloud across the cosmos, drift
down on fiesta-goers
everywhere. May they, too, perspire gray-
blue beads of gloom,
seething from their frolicking bowels up,
tequila-sangria-Prozac hangovers
smoldering like stick matches
stuffed and rubbing together
in their gritty hip pockets, as they each skip,
as animated as brandied flambé,
into a not-so-happy-go-lucky year-after!"

For Elizabeth Dear (Thank you, dear Elizabeth,
for introducing Zozo to Zarzo.)

THE COLDEST PLACE I'VE *EVER* BEEN

Do not let the palm trees fool you. Sacramento
merely *looks* more tropical than Great Falls,
Montana in late November
where it snows horizontally out of the north
and you don't dare glance up,
cocking your frosty nostrils toward Canada,
not without a thick mustache
shelterbelting your sinuses and cerebellum
from drifts, berms, cornices—
your brainpan from turning glacial—
and we're not talking Fourth of July child's play
Popsicle headaches here, no sirree. The coldest
place I've shivered me Popeye timbers in
is Sacramento—colder than bone
marrow of the reptilian soul cold, colder
than an Admiral Richard E. Byrd turd cold. So cold
your guardian angel wishes you harm
hoping to cinch a gig
with the other Big Boss. Trust me,
I know cold. Where the stork dropped my frost-
bitten bundle in the icy month of May,
it snows 300-plus,
you-better-flag-the-outhouse-like-a-sprinkler-head,
inches on the level every winter. I have shoveled
horizonless driveways, bottomless walks—tunneled my way
from the back door into white-hole infinity. I have
known from day one the definitive synonym
for "penitential abyss" is "Wisconsin winter," 50 below
windchill that, on one Good Friday,
grounded even you-know-Who. And in Montana,
the third coldest place I've ever been,

I've stood between house and hay barn
in the foothills of the Rockies, a minus 80
nor'easter covering my knee-deep tracks
the split second I stepped out of them—stood there
spellbound in a hoop-skirt of snow-
drift to my thighs. I might stand there still
were it not for the horses nickering
me out of my trance. So, you see, I know
Snow can be enchanting. But not
her blue-haired hoarfrost
of a wicked half-sister, Cold—most bitter
when she's forced to chaperone
their pantywaist second cousins, Rain and Fog,
to Sacramento, where my bewildered hosts,
oblivious to winter, because *"this is California,"*
won't, no matter how much I whine,
turn the thermostat up past friggin'-fifty-frigid-five!

For Nancy and Quinton, Sally and Sue

FEEDING HORSES IN RICHARD
HUGO'S FISHING PARKA

An easy swim-stroke every morning,
every evening, I float into the great
big man's coat, the thermometer
some days bottoming-out
at minus 50, but still not cold enough
to cut the khaki canvas and wool
lined with quilted pink
satin that slides
"lovingly," Dick might've said, over feather
vest and sweaters. Bundled
almost to the tops of my moon boots—
half-bales grappled under each arm,
pockets filling with alfalfa leaf—
I plod like an astronaut or deep-sea diver
in a late-night Anthony Quinn movie
Dick likely drank to once
with glee. He liked his westerns horseless,
and goddamn it anyway, on those days
when wind swirls low
slipping its frigid giant-squid fingers up
suddenly under this coat
as if I've broken all the way
to my armpits through ice
of a glacial lake we fished
until our Olys froze
mid-sip, us cursing in cracked Italian
our luckless quest for the fur-bearing trout—
on *those* days, I'm with Hugo
howling "…and to hell with horses, too!"

For Ripley

"...SO JUST HOW *DO* YOU STAND THE VICIOUS WINTERS?"

The forecasters swore on their weather balloons
swore in serious rhyme—"heavy and steady
so better get ready"—swore
the behemoth storm out of the north
was freight-training its way,
leaving its thick Canadian wake of blue
misery across The Medicine Line
into our balmy Montana lives. "Gospel, this time,"
I thought, betting the odds. So I split
a wheelbarrow heaped with cedar and pitch
pine kindling—grappled armload
upon armload of lodgepole
rounds and fir halves, stocked-up
on coffee, eggs, whiskey, bread (staples),
plus the makings of gravies, soups,
son-of-a-bitch stews, every rib-
sticking larder and pantry thing
slumgullion-able. I stacked alfalfa
bales close to the corrals
for speedy feeding, topped off the propane pig,
limbered-up my scoop-shovel stroke,
my 53-year-old 50-below-zero
zero-gravity arthritic astronaut
snowdrift plod in long johns,
insulated coveralls, wool-lined parka,
Sorrel packs. I wore the fleece
of six sheep, made sure I was
head-to-toe wind-resistant

and bulletproof to boot. I waited.
It hit. We embraced
like estranged twin brother sumos back in touch
with our feuding blood. We relived
the childhood tussle, fought bull-moose-
hard for the title of long-forbearance,
reveled in this rare fair-chase
vestige of free will and wonder. The storm
held its frozen-tundra ground
for weeks, tested every molecule, cell,
atom of my mettle. What it denied,
I defied. I phoned daily Arizona friends
one-hundred-and-fifty Fahrenheit degrees
less cold than I. It finally broke—just
a skosh before I almost grimaced *give*,
and so I grinned *gotcha* instead. Unfolding
its stiff wings, it flopped off
through the hoarfrost dawn, the chinook
arch hovering overhead like Starship
Enterprise on a clandestine mission
to varmint-hunt Klingons. I drank ice-
cold Guinness just for spite, sported
my Hawaiian surfer shirt, huarache sandals,
Carhartt coveralls knifed-off at the thighs,
gloated to the mercury rising, rising
right before my reptilian-red eyes,
past minus 20, zero, plus 35—

good-bye freezing point, hello thaw—
...and, by the way, the answer to your question is,
simply, my temperate-climate friend,
we just store our straw-hatted humility away
until spring, don layer upon itchy layer
of hubris over our thickened hides, and grit
our incisors against all chatter. That's how
we make the vicious Montana winters stand *us*.

For Lyle, Jared, and Tyler Meeks

Roaring With Metaphorical Fire

SMART MOUTH—MANDIBULAR PROGNATHISM*

** A condition where the lower jaw outgrows the upper—alleged to
have been derived from the princely Polish family of Mazovian Piasts.*

Novocain turning my face to stone, I learn
it's my last remaining wisdom
tooth Doctor Olsen is crowning
in porcelain—right side, right brain,
sanctum sanctorum, holy of holies,
the tabernacle, the cranial grail
frothing hot with creativity, and what is
creativity if not the infinite
rainbow bridge of wisdom between
body and soul? I'll gladly stroll
to my grave still grinding that day
whatever toil or torment
this perfect imperfect world
causes to stick in my craw, thanks
to the jut of my lower jaw,
my bulldog underbite
aligning my right upper
second molar with this
one bottom third molar
miraculously granted its sovereign stay
of execution on extraction day
decades back when Doc Odorizzi—army
airborne jumper of the Rhine
behind enemy lines and, thereafter,
deemer of fear as redeeming virtue—
must have incurred a lethargic lapse
into compassion.
             Soft food be damned,
I plan to exit this earth chewing

still on life's hardtack,
flossing with coarse mane hair
of a bronc. I'm going out kicking,
spitting into the hurricane eye
of ignorance. I'll not bow to
fiction or fact, to all the ballyhoo
and foofaraw, the flimflamming boogeyman
humbuggery, or the sheep's wool
pulled over our eyeteeth by queens,
high priests, presidents, kings,
soothsayers, succubi or tooth fairies
scamming to snatch our last
molars from beneath
deathbed's pillow soaked with drool,
with dreams unlived.
                    I *will* renounce Satan,
decay *and* gum disease. I'll gargle
daily with Mexican perfume—blue agave
tequila *reposado*—shower my wisdom
tooth in euphoric bright lights. I'll yodel
like a lone wolf rodeo poet soprano
extolling the arioso's holiest note,
my tongue tucked, head tilted back, crown
blinding with its brilliance
heaven's Mensa intelligentsia—them gaping
dumbfounded while regaling
in the scintillation of this royalty,
this epicurean jewel, this *numero* thirty-two
virtuoso oracle holding court,
ruling the roost, cock-a-doodle-
dooing until closing time
my loftiest thoughts from its deep-
rooted, four-legged stool at the end of the bar.

For George and the Gang, and for Doc John Martin

BIRTHDAY VIRTUE-OF-DEFIANCE RITUAL AFTER 60

I drop my cosmic drawers
to moon all of the dark
heinous forces
causing my fugacious body to wrinkle
and rot, in spite of the mind
still longing to blossom
its juiciest fruit, in spite of
the heart igniting yet
its most flamboyant
juvenescence, its sexiest
residues of joy. Screw you,
you perfidious Indian-giving
cryptic sons-a-bitches, you bamboozling
April Fools' Day wild-goose-chase
blasphemers of the Holy
Grail, you booby-trapping
Judases of the delusional we
en route to the Fountain of Youth—
screw you and the Newtonian
laws of sucked-off gravity
you flew in on: Hallelujah!
Hosanna! Kiss the Wrangler-
jeaned time-lapse eclipse
of my sagging sweet ass, *Amen*!

For Ed Groenendyke

ZARZYSKI STARS IN *FOOTBALL ZOMBIE APOCALYPSE NOW*

"I love the smell of napalm in the morning..."
Robert Duvall

Smelling of mothballs and mildewed youth,
of gridiron glory days buried alive
forty-two years ago, I—the delusional undead
duped into buying into that psychobabble
that "60 is the new 16"—
sport my Halloween orange and black
Hurley High letter jacket (fitting a little
like an O. J. Simpson glove)
exhumed from the dark
cobwebbed closet of my Boris Karloff-
Bela Lugosi horror movie youth. I haunt,
on game night, the goal-post-shadowed
Hurley Midgets end zone
I both defended *and scored in* and… yes,
damn-it, I *did say* "Midgets." Not Pipsqueaks,
Peewees, Munchkins, Half-pints. Not Homunculi. Not
even The Hurley Vertically-Challenged. But just
good old emphatically-oh-*so*-politically-
incorrect, **Midgets**!—as in, **GO-O-O Midgets**!
                                        A blast
from the fashionable past, thinks I, fantasizing
my-Midget-stud-self
strutting the hundred-yard hash-marked fashion runway—
modeling my eBay-able vintage regalia
from sports memorabilia yore…*until,*
blindsided by a gaggle of giggling girls
cutting a wide swath around me, I overhear,
"My grandpa, like, in his coffin last month,

wore, like, a totally weird letter jacket,
like, exactly like that!"
                              Let us now lay
forever to rest all dubious debate
as to the brutality of words
committing murder in the first. I am
chop-blocked, nonliving Zombie Zarzyski proof
that merciless words get their sick thrills
maiming first, killing later. Boneyard divots
dangling like decomposed flesh
off my *Pole*-axed psyche, off the sagging bill
of my **Mighty Midgets** ball cap, off the collapsed
number 72 of my harpooned hot-air balloon
heart, I pry what's left of my living-dead pride
back into a goal line stance. I punch-in
B-51, Sam the Sham and the Pharaohs,
spinning from the 45 grooves in the juke joint
Wurlitzer of my swirling frontal lobe
cuing me to lip sync my tit
for tat sexagenarian retaliation,
     "Hey there, Little Riding Hood,
       you sure are lookin' good,
       you're every*thang*
       a Big Bad Wolf could w*aaa*nt,
       OU-*OOOOOOOO!*
       (I mean, baa-a-a-a-)"—
toward the bling-butted Midg-ettes
hot-footing it away from me,
as if they'd just seen not just any old
moldy ghost, but a golden-oldies
rock-n-roll *Zombie* ghost! Oh, if only
they'd have feasted their nubile pupils
on this sinewy Polish-Italian
Homecoming King stallion

Midget in high-top Wilson spikes
back in '68.
            Dragging the ball
and chain of my phantasmagorical past
shackled to my one good ankle, I do
The Zombie-Hobble toward the Wasteland
of Anonymity, where, with my first sad limp
outside of Life's Stadium gate, I, on instinct,
buttonhook a 180 and shout
my magniloquent scrimmage line trash-talk
magnum opus, "**OH *YEAH?*...well
your no-doubt oom-pah-pah grandpa,
who can't even find his stupid-ass
marching band way out of an unlocked box,
can, like, totally eat a shovelful of mool
and bark at the stupid-ass tuba moon!**"
                              I jog off
gloating like the macho Robert Duvall-ski of *Football
Zombie Apocalypse Now* that I am. Wringing
my hands, my ecstatic finger bones click-
clacking like team spikes on pavement
between field and geriatric ward
after the last big win, I deliver,
to an awestruck audience of Zombie jocks,
the cinematic simile salvo of all time:
                        "Like
teen nectar, like teen sweat, like teen sex, like
the musky flux of gym-locker reminiscence
making its lustful comeback
in the mausoleum of the Zombie mind,
I *love* the smell of nostalgia in the evening—it
smells like...Midget Zarzyski victory."

For Greg Loreti, Tony Rodeghiero, and the Class of '69

TURKEY BUZZARDS CIRCLING NIRVANA

"Do not go gentle into that good night.
Rage, rage against the dying of the light."
Dylan Thomas

"Anything that ain't got some fighting in it
is like a funeral, and I don't like *funerals."*
John L. Sullivan

I'm fed up burying all my dead friends
never quite friend enough to hang tough
long enough to haul my carcass off. Who'll be left
to honor my last sons-a-bitching wishes, to tell how
I abhorred, more than weddings, this
boring ceremony with its slow crawl—land-barge
caravan of traffic jam sadness
led by death's ebony stretch limo,
the world's most crooked cabby
rolling at the speed of greed, six-digit
jockey-box meter spinning a-blur
faster than reels of a one-armed bandit. Speaking of
highway robbery, of watching death dry, *if*
anyone *is* still around, make my final ride
person-flaked flamed. Stir my coarse ash
into thirty coats of lacquer
sprayed over the blazing
orange of both '40s Merc doors. Paint me
roaring with metaphorical fire
down some one-horse-town's quarter mile. Punch it
while passing paper-sacked pints
of high school wine. Bravura
and fuel tanks overflowing, cruise
Hell's drag with its one lurid stoplight
beaming eternal, the Grim Reaper

glowering in the crosswalk. Screw him *and*
that Texas penknife he packs
in these computerized-nuke times. Swerve,
brush the anorectic booger back
to the curb—door him, moon him,
flip him off and leave him coughing
up his Hoover vacuum bag guts
in your burnt-rubber exhaust, your raucous
YEE-HAW! At *my* final cash-in and last blast-off
I want you jaspers to laugh
so hard you almost die, but don't—I want to
leave you believing there might be just one
more wild good-bye like this to live for.

For Jim Rooney

195

SHORT-BUT-NOT-*TOO*-SWEET EULOGY TO, *AND FROM*, THE ROCKIN' DOUBLE-Z *BARWHISKEY BIZARZYSKI CZARZYSKI* UNIPOET

Ars longa, vita brevis

Worshipped words
Spurred broncs
Incited friends
Indicted God.

Scorned jobs
Nurtured work
Suffered fools
Exalted earth.

Nourished birds
Feigned wealth
Reveled broke
Questioned self.

Savored food
Guzzled ink
Stage left
Let Us Drink!

The End

(In a porcine derriere!)

Acknowledgments

As always, my heartiest personal gratitude to Elizabeth Dear, who, over the past quarter century, was the first to lend an ear to rough-draft readings of most of these works. Without your love and encouragement, your artist sensibilities, Liz, none of this could have occurred as organically and harmoniously as it has. Thanks, as well, to additional household audience members, Zeke Zarzyski and Mister Mink. And to the passel of friends who participated in my title survey for this collection—thank goodness, for without your majority vote in favor of *Steering With My Knees*, I'd have likely gone with my business-decision hunch to call the booger *51 Shades of gray*. And to my publisher-editor, Allen Morris Jones, who belongs in the *Guinness World Records* under the category "Zen Master Stoicism Capacity For Megalomaniacal Polish-Mafioso-Rodeo-Poets." And to Rick DeMarinis and Larry Levinger—two of this planet's finest, and funniest, prose writers—for your friendship and feedback. *And*, speaking of friendship to the power of infinity, I bow with not just any painterly gratitude, but with *impasto fauvist* gratitude to you, Larry Pirnie, for echoing my rodeo-poetry fireworks with your volcanic buckin' hoss brush strokes, your veritable Hubble Telescope refractions—splashes, spurts, swashes, swirls, surges—of detonated colors, as well as with your remarkable section-partition images adding so much propulsion to this book. What an honor, what a thrill, to have lived in the wild presence of the covers' actual 24 x 48 inch canvas, since Liz and I first hung "Road To Hell" on our most prominent living room wall back in 2000.

Lastly and, therein, **emphatically**, I'm indebted up to the poetic elbow of my middle ear to an outside reader of exceptional editorial acumen and adeptness, Glenna Branagan. Glenna grew up, in the fifties and sixties, seventy-five miles north of Great Falls with her siblings Maryanne, Kathleen, Carmine, Colleen, Barbara—the Big Sandy, Montana *Erin Go Bragh* Branagan-Sister Sextet. The impetus behind my editing collaboration with Glenna occurred sometime in 2012 when I serendipitously crossed trails at the post office with an acquaintance, who I understood to work as a consultant and editor. When I asked if she'd been keeping busy, she divulged that she had just finished a project with a certain, esteemed Pulitzer Prize-winning novelist. I was surprised, as well as comforted, I suppose, to learn that even well-established literary figures seek assistance from outside their publishing houses—although, granted, I did not inquire if the involvement had to do with publicity, research, or actual editing. Solely in keeping with my own agenda—albeit hidden from even me at the time—I simply assumed the latter. For 37 years until his death in 2010, my dear friend and poet-extraordinaire, Quinton Duval, had fielded every poem I'd written. Since Quinton's passing, I've felt adrift—not at all confident that anyone could ever fulfill his capacity to harmonize with my *ars poetica* ear and sensibilities. The timely post office encounter made me ponder, however, the possibility of somebody in my circles of friends who might bring to the editorial table something different, yet, in a unique way, equally significant to that which Quinton so generously and honestly brought. Glenna's "non-poet," yet keenly musical, ear and eye, heart and soul, did precisely that, and then some. In fact, *because* her comments—addressing the introduction, addressing contributive characteristics (thematic, tonal, etc.) of individual poems or distinct passages therein, addressing the choreography and overall sustained "focal point" of this book—were seldom made from the pitcher's mound or home plate vantage points, but always from other key, strategic "positions" in the proverbial ballpark, I eventually learned to follow her cues *toward* things amiss rather than explicitly *of* things boldly marked amiss in red, so to speak? And, trust me, there is a difference. In the midst of this extremely fresh and adventurous editorial "communication," I discovered entrances to poetic passageways that would've otherwise remained cobwebbed over, unexplored. I can't say right now if this rapport would transcribe to any and every writing focus, but it rolled smoothly as the jeweled-watch workings of an ant hill on *this* project.

I'm forever indebted for the energy, enthusiasm, and, at times, "cantankerous" Irish candor that Glenna-the-Vehement (as I came to refer to her) brought to "the yard," to the diamond, to "the show," (yes, more baseball metaphor in tribute to the definitive poem of her life, her son Ryan, who, drafted by the Red Sox in 2006, currently stars for an Independent League team.) Thank you, Glenna—I will never peer into the front cover of this volume without seeing your name glowing from the shadows alongside mine.

Credits

The author and publisher extend their gratitude to the publishers who, most recently, printed a number of poems included and, in some cases, revised here: "Zarzyski Meets The Copenhagen Angel," "Dear Mom," "Zarzyski Stomachs the Oxford Special with Zimmer at the Ox Bar & Grill"—*Roughstock Sonnets*, The Lowell Press (1989).

"Flat Crick's Mad Gourmet Poet and His Fishing Fanatic Neighbor Hold the First-Ever Polecatting Derby," "Yevgeny Alexandrovich Yevtushenko: Cowboy Poet," "Why *I* Am Not Going to Buy a Computer"—*I Am Not A Cowboy*, Dry Crik Press (1995).

"Monte Carlo Express—P.O. Box 258, 15.3 Miles Home," "Escorting Grammy to the Potluck Rocky Mountain Oyster Feed at Bowman's Corner," "Martini McRae & Whisky Zarzyski: A Brace of Blackjact Aces," "How the Lord Throwed-In with Mom to Make Me Quit the Broncs," "Benny Reynolds' Bareback Riggin," "The Roughstockaholic's 'Just-One-More-Last-One' Blues," "A Cowboy Reel," "Ain't No Life After Rodeo…," "The Heavyweight Champion Pie-Eatin' Cowboy of the West"—*All This Way For The Short Ride*, The Museum of New Mexico Press (1996).

"Bingo in the Church Basement," "Riding Double: 16 & Beating the Heat," "Hurley High," "Why I Like Butte…," "Linguistics"—*Blue-Collar Light*, Red Wing Press (1998).

"Cowboys & Indians," "The Tumbleweed Munchies," "*Bizarzyski—Mad Bard and Carpenter Savant of Manchester, Montana—Feeds the Finicky Birds*," "Antipasto," "Potatoes"—*Wolf Tracks On The Welcome Mat*, Oreanabooks / Carmel Publishing (2003).

"Riding Double Wild," "Photo Finish," "*Long Sagebrush Drives…*," "The Ms. of the Mega-Munitions," "Sadly—Oh-so-Sadly—I Have to Explain *The Sopranos* to Someone Who Just Does Not *Capice*," "Smart Mouth," "Turkey Buzzards Circling Nirvana"—*51: 30 Poems, 20 Lyrics, 1 Self-Interview*, Bangtail Press (2011).

"After Sipping Chardonnay and Talking Art, Tossin' Shots Poetically at Doc Holliday's," "Birthday Virtue-of-Defiance Ritual after 60," "Telemarketer Malediction," "Why I Ain't Buying Into the Word, 'Inspiration',"—Limited Edition Mini-Anthologies, Bunchgrass Press (2012-13).

A good number of these poems have also been recorded under the following CD titles: *Rock 'n' Rowel* (2006). Open Path Music—Gordon Stevens, Tim Volpicella, Lee Ray, Scott Sorkin, Producers; *The Glorious Commotion of It All* (2003) and *Words Growing Wild* (1998). Jim Rooney Productions—Jim Rooney, Producer; *Ain't No Life After Rodeo* (1992). Horse Sense Productions—Justin Bishop, Producer.

Title Index

About the Author

Paul Zarzyski left his Hurley, Wisconsin home ground in the fall of '73 for Missoula, where he studied creative writing at the University of Montana with Richard Hugo, Madeline DeFrees, and John Haines, received his MFA degree, and later taught Dick's classes after his passing. While teaching in The Program and riding bareback broncs on the ProRodeo Circuit, he attended in 1987 the first of his twenty-eight consecutive National Cowboy Poetry Gatherings in Elko, Nevada. He's made his living since as a performance poet at venues that include The Library of Congress, The Kennedy Center Millennium Stage, The Australian Stockman's Hall of Fame, Festival Hall in London, and The Mother Lode Theater in Butte, where he was featured in 1999 on Garrison Keillor's "A Prairie Home Companion." He's appeared, as well, with the Reno Philharmonic Orchestra and the Spokane Symphony. Imbued with Richard Hugo's belief that poetry *is* music, Paul has also applied his poetics to the art of lyric writing and has co-written songs with esteemed musicians Tom Russell, Ian Tyson, David Wilkie of Cowboy Celtic, Wylie Gustafson, Don Edwards, and others. The author of twelve books, chapbooks, and limited-edition chapbooks—most recently, *51: 30 Poems, 20 Lyrics, 1 Self-Interview* (Bangtail Press, 2011)—and five spoken-word CD recordings, Paul's life's work was celebrated with the 2005 Montana Governor's Arts Award for Literature. He currently lives west of Great Falls with art historian and C. M. Russell scholar, Elizabeth Dear, their Aussie dog, Zeke, and horses Pecos and Lash.

CPSIA information can be obtained
at www.ICGtesting.com
Printed in the USA
FFOW01n1353180118
44363776-44054FF

9 780962 378997